Pocket
LOS ANGELES

TOP SIGHTS • LOCAL LIFE • MADE EASY

Adam Skolnick

In This Book

QuickStart Guide

Your keys to understanding the city – we help you decide what to do and how to do it

Need to Know
Tips for a smooth trip

Neighborhoods
What's where

Explore Los Angeles

The best things to see and do, neighborhood by neighborhood

Top Sights
Make the most of your visit

Local Life
The insider's city

The Best of Los Angeles

The city's highlights in handy lists to help you plan

Best Walks
See the city on foot

Best...
The best experiences

Survival Guide

Tips and tricks for a seamless, hassle-free city experience

Getting Around
Travel like a local

Essential Information
Including where to stay

Our selection of Los Angeles' best places to eat, drink and experience:

◎ **Sights**

⊗ **Eating**

⊖ **Drinking**

✪ **Entertainment**

⊕ **Shopping**

These symbols give you the vital information for each listing:

☎	Telephone Numbers	⊹	Family-Friendly
⊙	Opening Hours	☻	Pet-Friendly
Ⓟ	Parking	☐	Bus
⊗	Nonsmoking	☐	Ferry
@	Internet Access	Ⓜ	Metro
⊚	Wi-Fi Access	Ⓢ	Subway
⊿	Vegetarian Selection	⊖	London Tube
⌖	English-Language Menu	⊡	Tram
		⊡	Train

Find each listing quickly on maps for each neighborhood:

Bar Hemingway

16 ⊖ Map p233, B2

Legend has it that Hemi self, wielding a machine erate this timber-pan ered bar during showpiece is a en by Papa ar town. Dress s.com; Hôtel Rit ; ⊙6.30pm-2a

6 ◎ Plac

Lonely Planet's Los Angeles

Lonely Planet Pocket Guides are designed to get you straight to the heart of the city.

Inside you'll find all the must-see sights, plus tips to make your visit to each one really memorable. We've split the city into easy-to-navigate neighborhoods and provided clear maps so you'll find your way around with ease. Our expert authors have searched out the best of the city: walks, food, nightlife and shopping, to name a few. Because you want to explore, our 'Local Life' pages will take you to some of the most exciting areas to experience the real Los Angeles.

And of course you'll find all the practical tips you need for a smooth trip: itineraries for short visits, how to get around, and how much to tip the guy who serves you a drink at the end of a long day's exploration.

It's your guarantee of a really great experience.

Our Promise

You can trust our travel infor- mation because Lonely Planet authors visit the places we write about, each and every edition. We never accept freebies for positive coverage, so you can rely on us to tell it like it is.

QuickStart Guide 7

Explore Los Angeles 21

Worth a Trip:

The Best of Los Angeles 157

Los Angeles' Best Walks

Los Angeles' Best...

Survival Guide 177

QuickStart Guide

Welcome to Los Angeles

LA runs deeper than the blonde beaches and celebrified hills would have you believe. It's a beacon for small-town dreamers, an open-minded angel best defined by simple, life-affirming moments – a cracked-ice, Jazz Age cocktail on Beverly Blvd or a hike high into the Hollywood Hills sagebrush. And the night music. There is always night music.

Amoeba Music store (p38), Hollywood
JAMES KIRKIKIS/GETTY IMAGES ©

Los Angeles
Top Sights

Hollywood Boulevard & the Hollywood Walk of Fame (p24)

In LA stars are more visible on-screen, in high-end restaurants and embedded in this speckled sidewalk than they are in the hazy night sky.

Griffith Observatory & Hollywood Sign
(p42)

Two iconic sights dominate the Hollywood Hills ridgeline. One is a stylish window onto the universe. The other needs no introduction.

Getty Center
(p68)

The Getty Center presents triple delights: a stellar art collection (Renaissance to David Hockney), Richard Meier's cutting-edge architecture and truly captivating seasonal gardens.

La Brea Tar Pits & Page Museum
(p72)

Deep beneath Wilshire Blvd is a gooey treasure trove of crude oil and tusks and bones, where thousands of ice-age creatures perished between 10,000 and 40,000 years ago.

Los Angeles County Museum of Art (p74)

LACMA is not just LA's premier museum, it's a vortex of art, jazz, film and culture not to be missed.

Santa Monica Pier & Beach (p90)

Santa Monica's essential landmark is absolutely unmissable and best experienced at its very edge, where waves lap against the barnacled pylons, as golden sand unfurls north and south.

URBAN LIGHT BY CHRIS BURDEN. IMAGE RICHARD CUMMINS/GETTY IMAGES ©

RICHARD CUMMINS/GETTY IMAGES ©

Venice Boardwalk (p106)

There is only one Venice Beach, and the Boardwalk is where she lets her freak flag fly. Be prepared to encounter the bohemian and the bizarre.

Walt Disney Concert Hall (p120)

Where brilliant music meets virtuoso architecture. Take a bow, Mr Gehry. You make the LA Philharmonic look and sound so very good.

Universal Studios (p142)

The magic of moviemaking gets its due at ever-popular Universal, one of the world's oldest continuously operating motion-picture studios and theme parks.

Malibu (p102)

A moneyed but still laid-back beach town, Malibu rambles along the Pacific Coast Hwy for 27 gorgeous miles blessed with stunning coastal mountains, pristine coves and epic waves.

ALBERT VALLES/GETTY IMAGES ©

© DISNEY

Exposition Park (p136)

A rose garden, vintage rocket ships, a space shuttle, dozens of dinosaurs and more can be found in this wonderful collection of museums and grounds near the USC campus.

Disneyland & Disney California Adventure (p150)

The Happiest Place on Earth is an 'imagineered' utopia where both staff and visitors are forever upbeat, the thrills are wholesome and there's a parade every day.

Los Angeles
Local Life

Insider tips to help you find the real city

LA is more a neighborhood quilt than a traditional metropolis, so in your haste to explore LA's best-known barrios, don't forget to sample the out-of-the-way corners, too. Hidden treasures await.

Cruising Echo Park (p52)

▶ Echo Park Lake
▶ Short Stop

Echo Park is one of LA's old-school, working-class, multi-ethnic neighborhoods, and home to an emerging and intriguing creative subculture.

Gallery Hopping in Culver City (p86)

▶ Art galleries
▶ Sidewalk cafes

A decade ago Culver City bloomed from its bland, quasi-suburban, studio-town roots into a stylish yet unpretentious destination for fans of art, culture and food. The recession was a stumbling block, but these days it's better than ever.

Manhattan Beach, Beyond the Sand (p116)

▶ Beach living
▶ Gastropubs

The wide beach dotted with string bikinis and bronzed surfers riding consistent waves will lure you in, but the area's surprising kitchens will nourish your soul.

Shopping the Fashion District (p122)

▶ Sample sales
▶ People-watching

Bargain hunters love this 100-block warren of fashion. Deals can be found but the district's size and selection can be as bewildering as seeing sassy fashionistas wandering among mumbling drunks with neck tattoos in a perma-haze.

Pasadena (p138)

▶ Museums
▶ Local history

Pasadena is a brainy, preppy small town in a big city that will open your mind and touch your soul if you let it. Hit the museums, see a jazz combo, grab a bite. Repeat.

Echo Park Lake (p53)

Manhattan Beach (p116)

Other great places to experience the city like a local:

Hollywood Farmers Markets (p32)

Musso & Frank Grill (p34)

Griffith Park (p47)

Hammer Museum (p58)

Yakitoriya (p62)

Larchmont Ave (p82)

Santa Monica Markets (p98)

Annenberg Community Beach House (p100)

Staples Center (p134)

Los Angeles
Day Planner

Day One

Begin your day in West Hollywood with a quick breakfast at **Joan's on Third** (p80) before perusing the boutiques on Beverly Blvd, Melrose Pl and Melrose Ave.

Drive north on Laurel Canyon, then head west on Mulholland Dr and stop at the **Getty Center** (p68), where you can glimpse fine art, stunning gardens and epic views. Then keep pushing west to the **Venice Boardwalk** (p106) for sunset.

After a sunset beach stroll, find your way to Venice's trendy **Abbot Kinney** (p109) shopping district, where you can hit **Gjelina** (p109) for a fantastic dinner of creative small plates and thin-crust pizza. Then double back to Hollywood for rum and burlesque at **La Descarga** (p33).

Day Two

Day two is all about the east side, so start with breakfast downtown at **Eggslut** (p130) before hitting the **Grammy Museum** (p126) for some harmonic time-travel. Then it's on to **MOCA** (p126), where you may lose yourself in color and form, before a stunning lunch at **Sushi Gen** (p131) in Little Tokyo.

Shop your way through Sliver Lake and Los Feliz. You'll enjoy exploring the many edgy fashion and vintage boutiques on Hillhurst, Vermont and Sunset, and don't forget to pause at **Spitfire Girl** (p51).

Grab a bite at **Jitlada** (p31) in Thai Town before catching a show at the **Upright Citizens Brigade** (p35) or swilling craftsman cocktails at **No Vacancy** (p33).

Short on time?
We've arranged Los Angeles' must-sees into these day-by-day itineraries to make sure you see the very best of the city in the time you have available.

Day Three

It's time to soak up the sun, sand and the Pacific blue, so fuel up with a proper American breakfast at **Uncle Bill's Pancake House** (p117) in Manhattan Beach before making your way up the coast and onto the **Venice Boardwalk** (p106).

The **Santa Monica Pier** (p90) should be coming into view, so take a picture among the anglers at the edge then stroll along **Santa Monica Beach** (p90), or continue up the coast and into Malibu, where you can watch the sun set beyond Point Dume at **Westward Beach** (p103).

Now that the sun has dropped, it's time to loop south back into Santa Monica, where you can get a superb meal at **Rustic Canyon** (p96) before stopping for a drink at **Basement Tavern** (p98).

Day Four

Day four is about filling the gaps, so after an indie industry breakfast at **Square One** (p32), take your time and appreciate the greatness that is **LACMA** (p74). If the kids get bored, consider a diversion to the **La Brea Tar Pits** and the **Page Museum** (p72) before lunching at the original **Farmers Market** (p81).

Hit **Rodeo Dr** (p65) for a blast of Beverly Hills bling before exploring the (much!) less sophisticated jumble that is **Melrose Ave** (p58), between Fairfax and La Brea. Skaters should head south on Fairfax to where skate culture and hip-hop collide.

After dark, grab dim sum at **Pingtung** (p62) and see a show at the **El Rey** (p82), **Hollywood Bowl** (p28) or the **Echo** (p53).

Need to Know

For more information,
see Survival Guide (p178)

Currency
US dollar ($)

Visas
The US Visa Waiver Program allows visitors from 38 countries to arrive without a visa. Visitors from elsewhere must secure a tourist visa in advance.

Money
ATMs are widely available and credit cards are accepted in all hotels and most restaurants.

Cell Phones
International cell (mobile) phones will work with roaming. Some unlocked GSM phones will work with local SIMs.

Time
Pacific Standard Time (PST; UTC/GMT minus eight hours) Nov to mid-Mar; Pacific Daylight Savings Time (PDT; UTC/GMT minus seven hours) mid-Mar to Oct.

Plugs & Adaptors
LA area outlets demand the North American 20A/120V grounded plug.

Tipping
Tipping is considered mandatory for sit-down, full-service meals. The minimum tip should be 15-20%. Tip bartenders, too ($1 per drink will suffice).

① Before You Go

Your Daily Budget

Budget less than $100
- ► Dorm beds from $35
- ► Excellent supermarkets for self-catering
- ► Ample free concerts and events

Midrange $150–250
- ► Midrange sleeping options from $120
- ► Two-course dinner and glass of wine $40
- ► Night out with live music from $50

Top end from $250
- ► Sleeping options from $250
- ► Lunch and drinks at industry haunt $75 and up

Useful Websites

Lonely Planet (www.lonelyplanet.com/usa/los-angeles) Destination information, hotel bookings, traveler forum.

Los Angeles Downtown News (www.ladowntownnews.com) If it works, eats, drinks or sleeps downtown, they have the scoop.

LA Weekly (www.laweekly.com) LA's trusted indie news and culture rag.

Advance Planning

Three months before Book your hotel and rental car, and secure concert tickets.

One month before Buy tickets for exhibition openings at LACMA or MOCA.

One week before Reserve a table at any top-tier restaurant, and make reservations for high-demand bars and clubs such as No Vacancy.

② Arriving in Los Angeles

Los Angeles is more spread out than most major cities, and although there is a vibrant downtown, it's rather compact and LA is not. In fact, the city is a quilt with several self-contained neighborhoods knitted together, and transport details within and between them varies.

✈ From Los Angeles International Airport (LAX)

Destination	Best Transport
Hollywood, Silver Lake	Metro bus 42, Metro Red Line
Downtown	Metro Red Line, Flyaway Union Station
West Hollywood, Mid-City	Flyaway Westwood, Metro 20/720, Metro 4
Santa Monica	BBB 3
Venice	BBB 3, CC 1
Culver City	Flyaway Westwood, BBB 12
Burbank, Universal City	Flyaway Union Station, Metrolink

③ Getting Around

LA has an automobile pathos. Meaning almost everyone who lives here owns a car, and wishes they had a better one. However, there are multiple public transport options that link up and overlap throughout the LA area.

Ⓜ Metro & Metrolink

The Metro subway system is ever-expanding and links downtown LA with Hollywood, Koreatown, Pasadena, Long Beach, LAX, Culver City and, beginning in 2015, Santa Monica. It also connects with Metrolink light-rail service to Burbank and Orange County.

🚌 Bus

The best bus services are offered by LA's Metropolitan Transit Authority (MTA; 📞323-466-3876; www.metro.net; fares from $1.75), which has a handy trip planner on its website, and Santa Monica's Big Blue Bus (📞310-451-5444; www.bigbluebus.com; fares start from $1).

🚖 Taxi

Taxis are quite expensive and should only be used between nearby destinations. Uber (www.uber.com), the on-demand car service which allows you to order and pay for a ride via a smartphone app, is quite popular and useful here.

Los Angeles
Neighborhoods

Burbank & Universal City (p140)
Home to a theme park, Sushi Row and most of LA's major movie studios. It's also the birthplace of car culture and porn.

⊙ Top Sights
Universal Studios

West Hollywood & Beverly Hills (p54)
Big dollars and gay fabulous, wonderful shopping, sinful eateries and terrific nightlife too. From here you can explore the entire city.

Santa Monica (p88)
Mix with the surf rats, skate punks, yoga freaks, psychics and street performers along a stretch of sublime coastline.

⊙ Top Sights
Santa Monica Pier & Beach

⊙ Getty Center

LACMA

Venice (p104)
Inhale an incense-scented whiff of Venice, a boho beach town and longtime haven for artists, New Agers and free spirits.

⊙ Top Sights
Venice Boardwalk

Santa Monica ⊙
Pier & Beach

Venice ⊙
Boardwalk

Griffith Park, Silver Lake & Los Feliz (p40)

Where hipsters and yuppies collide in an immense urban playgound crowned with a window onto the universe.

Top Sights

Griffith Observatory & Hollywood Sign

Downtown (p118)

Historical, multilayered and fascinating, it's become so cool that the likes of *GQ* have called it America's best downtown.

Top Sights

Walt Disney Concert Hall

Worth a Trip

Top Sights

Disneyland & Disney California Adventure

Malibu

Getty Center

Exposition Park

Miracle Mile & Mid-City (p70)

Museum Row is the big draw, but funky Fairfax and the old Farmers Market are worthy destinations.

Top Sights

La Brea Tar Pits & Page Museum

LACMA

Hollywood (p22)

The nexus of the global entertainment industry offers starry sidewalks, blingy nightclubs and celebrity sightings.

Top Sights

Hollywood Boulevard & the Hollywood Walk of Fame

---

niversal tudios

Griffith Observatory & Hollywood Sign

Hollywood Boulevard & the Hollywood Walk of Fame

La Brea Tar Pits & Page Museum

Walt Disney Concert Hall

Exposition Park

Explore
Los Angeles

Oceanfront strand, Manhattan Beach (p116)
IAN LOGAN/GETTY IMAGES ©

Explore

Hollywood

The neighborhood most synonymous with LA, Hollywood's rise to stardom began with a 1920s ad campaign for Hollywoodland, a residential hillside development with its name announced to the world with towering white letters. Here are red-carpet premieres, bustling restaurants and bars, and a funky, endearing Thai Town.

The Sights in a Day

☀ Grab a gourmet breakfast at **Square One** (p32), then follow the stars on Hollywood Blvd with mandatory photo ops at **TCL Chinese Theatre** (p25), the **Dolby Theatre** (p25) and the **Hollywood Wax Museum** (p29).

☼ Break for lunch at **Jitlada** (p31), where you can also get a whiff of Hollywood's incredibly authentic Thai Town. If it's a sunny day, enjoy an outdoor beverage at the **Cat & Fiddle** (p34).

☽ Order a Mario Batali–imagined pizza at **Pizzeria Mozza** (p30), before catching a superb sketch-comedy show at **Upright Citizens Brigade** (p35). Unless, of course, you have tickets for a show at the **Hollywood Bowl** (p28) – a Hollywood evening that trumps all others.

 Top Sights

Hollywood Boulevard & the Hollywood Walk of Fame (p24)

♥ **Best of Los Angeles**

Eating
Pizzeria & Osteria Mozza (p30)
Jitlada (p31)

Drinking
No Vacancy (p33)
Harvard & Stone (p35)

Entertainment
Hollywood Bowl (p28)
Fonda Theatre (p35)

Getting There

Ⓜ **Metro** Hollywood is well connected to downtown and Universal City by the Metro Red Line.

Ⓜ **Metro** The most centrally located Red Line stops are Hollywood/Vine and Hollywood/Highland.

🚌 **Bus** MTA, LA's principal transit authority, connects Hollywood with all other parts of town.

Top Sights
Hollywood Boulevard & the Hollywood Walk of Fame

Hollywood Blvd is one of the most famous of LA's avenues thanks to the glitterati embedded into that speckled sidewalk. Big Bird, Bob Hope and Marilyn Monroe are among the stars worshipped, photographed and stepped on on the Hollywood Walk of Fame. Since 1960 more than 2400 performers – from legends to long-forgotten players – have been honored with a pink-marble sidewalk star. The galaxy extends from Hollywood Blvd and La Brea Ave to Gower St, and south along Vine St.

👁 Map p26, C3

www.walkoffame.com

Ⓜ Hollywood Blvd

Sidewalk star on the Hollywood Walk of Fame

Don't Miss

TCL Chinese Theatre

Stand in the footprints of silver-screen legends such as George Clooney in the courtyard of this grand movie palace, built in 1927 and formerly known as Grauman's Chinese Theatre. **TCL Chinese Theatre** (☎323-463-9576; www.tclchinese theatres.com; 6925 Hollywood Blvd; tours & movie tickets adult/child/senior $13.50/6.50/11.50) was inspired by Chinese imperial architecture, and the decor extends from the intricate courtyard to the ornate interior.

Dolby Theatre

The Academy Awards are handed out at the **Dolby Theatre** (www.dolbytheatre.com; 6801 Hollywood Blvd; tours adult/child, senior & student $17/12; ⊙10:30am-4pm), which also hosts other big events such as the *American Idol* finals. On the tour you get to sniff around the auditorium, admire a VIP room and see Oscar up close.

Janes House

The **Janes House** (6541 Hollywood Blvd) is the last remaining Victorian home on Hollywood Blvd. It was built in 1903 and was the former site of Miss Janes' School, which was attended by the children of old Hollywood icons such as Cecil B DeMille, Douglas Fairbanks and Charlie Chaplin. Nowadays? Um, it's a down-market mini-mall.

☑ Top Tips

▶ You can explore the boulevard by day, but it feels so much richer at night when the stars glitter and the sidewalk stains are (somewhat) hidden.

▶ New stars are born every two or three months, and include a public unveiling by the stars themselves.

▶ There's plenty of kitsch and worse to wade through on what scientists have determined to be among the cheesiest boulevards known to man, but there is also greatness lurking. Exhibit A: Musso & Frank's (p34) martinis. Exhibit B: Loteria Grill's (p31) tequila bar.

✗ Take a Break

Thai Town – a small section of Hollywood Blvd that's packed with tasty, spicy kitchens – is but a short drive east down the Boulevard. We love **Jitlada** (p31) for southern Thai specialties and **Ganda** (p33) for Bangkok-style street food.

A | B | C | D

1

Runyon
Canyon
Park

For reviews see
- ◉ Top Sights — p24
- ◎ Sights — p28
- ✖ Eating — p30
- 🍷 Drinking — p33
- 🎭 Entertainment — p35
- 🔒 Shopping — p38

Cahuenga
Blvd W

39

Hollywood
Bowl

Hollywood Bowl Rd

1

2

N Cahuenga Blvd

Hollywood
Bowl Museum

Hollywood
Fwy

Camrose Dr

6

Hollywood
Heritage
Museum

Grace Ave

2

Hillcrest Rd

Scenic
Gardens
Ave

Sycamore Ave

Franklin Ave

Whitely Ave

Franklin Ave

N Fuller Ave

Hollywood
Franklin
Park

Hollywood **Franklin Ave** Hollywood &
Highland

Yucca St

Franklin Ave

TMZ **Hollywood/** Hollywood
Tours **Highland** Wax
11 Ⓜ ⓘ ◎ 9 Museum 7

13 22

24

Hollywood Blvd

27

**Hollywood Boulevard
& the Hollywood
Walk of Fame**

43 5 ◎ 10

Hollywood
Museum

38

26

Guinness World
Records Museum

16 40

Selma Ave

4

20

17

N Gardner St

42

30

W Sunset Blvd

21

47

N Martel Ave

28

44

N Gardner St

N Vista St

N Martel Ave

N Fuller Ave

N Poinsettia Pl

N Alta Vista Blvd

N Formosa Ave

N Detroit St

N La Brea Ave

N Orange Dr

N Mansfield Ave

N Highland Ave

De Longpre Ave

Delongpre
Park

Homeland Ave

N Cahuenga Blvd

Ivar Ave

4

Plummer
Park

Fountain Ave

Lexington Ave

Hollywood
Recreation
Center

Santa Monica Blvd

Poinsettia
Recreation
Center

Warner
Hollywood
Studios

Willoughby Ave

N Vista St

N Poinsettia Pl

N Orange Dr

N Mansfield Ave

N Highland Ave

N Sycamore Ave

Romaine St

N Hudson Ave

Wilcox Ave

Cole Ave

5

12

15

E

F

G

H

Griffith Park

N Beachwood Dr

N 0 500 m
0 0.25 miles

HOLLYWOOD HILLS

Vine St

Argyle Ave

N Gower St

N Bronson Ave

Hollywood Fwy

Franklin Ave

Canyon Dr

N Van Ness Ave

Taft Ave

N Wilton Pl

Garfield Pl

N Western Ave

Franklin Ave

Russell Ave

N Kingsley Dr

⊗19
32 ✪ 🚇31

N Vine St

Hollywood Fwy

Capitol Records Tower

Yucca St

Carlos Ave

Hollywood Fwy

45
🔒

46
🏛️

29
🏛️

Hollywood Blvd

🅜 Hollywood/Vine
8

Hollywood & Vine

25
🚇

✪
33

Carlton Way

W St Andrews Pl

Hollywood/Western
🅜

N Serrano Ave

N Hobart Blvd

N Kingsley Dr

14
⊗

34

CBS Studios

W Sunset Blvd

HOLLYWOOD

Afton Pl

N Gower St

N Beachworth Dr

Gordon St

Tamarind Ave

N Bronson Ave

N Van Ness Ave

La Mirada Ave

St Andrews Pl

Fountain Ave

18
⊗

6
⊘

Lexington Ave

Lexington Ave

Virginia Ave

23
🚇

Virginia Ave

N Oxford Ave

Santa Monica Blvd

Eleanor Ave

N Vine St

Beth Olam Memorial Park

3
⊙

Hollywood Forever Cemetery

N Ridgewood Pl

Lemon Grove Recreation Center

1

2

3

4

5

Sights

Hollywood Bowl
LANDMARK

1 ⊙ Map p26, C1

Summers in LA just wouldn't be the same without this chill spot for music under the stars, from symphonies to big-name acts such as Baaba Maal, Sigur Ros, Radiohead and Paul McCartney. A huge natural amphitheater, the Hollywood Bowl has been around since 1922 and has great sound. (www.hollywoodbowl.com; 2301 Highland Ave; rehearsals free, performance costs vary; ⊙Apr-Sep; **P**)

Hollywood Bowl Museum
MUSEUM

2 ⊙ Map p26, C1

The Bowl, as it's affectionately known around town, enjoys a glamorous history, and this is where you can literally listen to it and watch it. Classic Bowl moments are yours thanks to audio and video footage of folks like the Beatles, the Stones and Mr James Hendrix. (www.hollywoodbowl.com/event/museum.cfm; admission free; ⊙10am-showtime Mon-Sat, 4pm-showtime Sun Jun-Sep, 10am-5pm Tue-Fri Oct-May)

Hollywood Forever Cemetery
CEMETERY

3 ⊙ Map p26, F5

Hollywood Forever boasts lavish landscaping, over-the-top tombstones, epic mausoleums and a roll call of departed superstars. Residents include Cecil B DeMille, Rudolph Valentino, femme fatale Jayne Mansfield and punk-rock icons Johnny and Dee Dee Ramone. For a full list pick up a map ($5) at the flower shop (9am to 5pm). (☎323-469-1181; www.hollywoodforever.com; 6000 Santa Monica Blvd; ⊙8am-5pm; **P**)

Capitol Records Tower
LANDMARK

4 ⊙ Map p26, E3

You'll recognize this iconic 1956 tower, one of LA's great modern-era buildings. Designed by Welton Becket, it resembles a stack of records topped by a stylus blinking out 'Hollywood' in Morse code. Garth Brooks and John Lennon have their stars outside. (1750 N Vine St; admission free)

Hollywood Museum
MUSEUM

5 ⊙ Map p26, C3

We quite like this musty temple to the stars, crammed with kitsch posters, costumes and rotating props. The museum is housed inside the handsome 1914 art deco Max Factor Building, where the make-up pioneer once worked his magic on Marilyn Monroe and Judy Garland. (☎323-464-7776; www.thehollywoodmuseum.com; 1660 N Highland Ave; adult/child $15/5; ⊙10am-5pm Wed-Sun)

Hollywood Heritage Museum
MUSEUM

6 ⊙ Map p26, C2

Hollywood's first feature-length film, Cecil B DeMille's *The Squaw Man*, was

Hollywood Museum

shot in this building in 1913–14, originally set at the corner of Selma and Vine Sts. DeMille went on to co-found Paramount and had the barn moved to the lot in the '20s. Now the Hollywood Heritage Museum, it's filled with a great collection of costumes, projectors and cameras from the early days of movie making. (www.hollywoodheritage. org; 2100 N Highland Ave; adult/child under 12 yr/senior $7/free/5; ⏰noon-4pm Wed-Sun)

Hollywood Wax Museum MUSEUM

7 ◎ Map p26, C3

Starved for celeb sightings? Don't fret: at this museum Angelina Jolie, Halle Berry and other red-carpet royalty will stand still – very still – for your camera. This retro haven of kitsch and camp has been around for over 40 years. (☎323-462-5991; www.hollywood wax.com; 6767 Hollywood Blvd; adult/child/ senior $17/9/15; ⏰10am-midnight; ♿)

Hollywood & Vine LANDMARK

8 ◎ Map p26, E3

If you turned on the radio in the 1920s and '30s, chances were you'd hear a broadcast 'brought to you from Hollywood and Vine.' These days a W hotel and a metro stop, and occasional block parties hosted by *Jimmy Kimmel Live*, keep this corner relevant.

Hollywood & Highland

MALL

9 Map p26, C3

It's apropos that a Disneyfied shopping mall would be the spark for Hollywood Blvd's rebirth. A marriage of kitsch and commerce, the main showpiece is a triumphal arch inspired by DW Griffith's 1916 movie *Intolerance,* which frames the Hollywood sign. (www.hollywood andhighland.com; 6801 Hollywood Blvd; admission free; ⏰10am-10pm Mon-Sat, to 7pm Sun)

Guinness World Records Museum

MUSEUM

10 Map p26, C3

You know the drill: the Guinness is all about the fastest, tallest, biggest, fattest and other superlatives. (www.guinnessmuseumhollywood.com; 6764 Hollywood Blvd; adult/child/senior $17/9/15; ⏰10am-midnight; 👪)

TMZ Tours

HOLLYWOOD TOUR

11 Map p26, B3

Cut the shame, do you really want to spot celebrities, glimpse their homes, and gawk and laugh at their dirt? Join this branded tour imagined by the paparazzi made famous. Tours are two hours long, and you will likely meet some of the TMZ stars and perhaps even celebrity guests on the bus! (☎855-4TMZ-TOUR; www.tmz.com/tour; 6925 Hollywood Blvd; adult/child $55/45; ⏰approx 10 tours daily)

Eating

Pizzeria & Osteria Mozza

ITALIAN $$$

12 Map p26, C5

Osteria Mozza is all about fine cuisine crafted from market-fresh, seasonal ingredients. Being a Mario Batali joint, you can expect adventure (squid-ink *chitarra freddi* with Dungeness crab, sea urchin and jalapeño) and consistent excellence. Pizzeria Mozza next door is (much) more laid-back and less expensive. Thin-crust pies come with squash blossoms and mozzarella, among other delights. Reservations are recommended. (☎323-297-0100; www.mozza-la.com; 6602

Top Tip

Hollywood Bowl

The Hollywood Bowl (p28) is the summer home of the LA Philharmonic and the Hollywood Bowl Orchestra. Eavesdrop on free rehearsals usually held from 9am to noon on Tuesday, Wednesday and Friday during the season.

Parking is free during the day, but expensive and limited on performance nights. Save yourself the headache and take a shuttle, such as the one running from Hollywood & Highland, which costs $5 per person round-trip.

Come early to claim a table for a pre-show picnic (alcohol permitted). There are concessions if you don't want to lug your own grub.

Melrose Ave; pizzas $11-19, dinner mains $27-38; ⊙pizzeria noon-midnight daily, osteria 5:30-11pm Mon-Fri, 5-11pm Sat, 5-10pm Sun)

Loteria Grill MEXICAN $$

 13 Map p26, D3

Spawned from the long-running, widely loved Farmers Market taco stand of the same name, this version offers elegant ambience, a ceviche bar, and a range of classic Mexican mains. The bar staff pour over 80 premium tequilas. (☎323-465-2500; www.loteriagrill. com; 6627 Hollywood Blvd; tacos $3-9, mains $16-23; ⊙11am-11pm Mon-Thu, to midnight Fri & Sat, 9am-11pm Sun; [P])

Jitlada THAI $$

14 Map p26, H3

A transporting taste of southern Thailand. Its crab curry and fried *som tum* (fried papaya salad) are fantastic, and they even have a Thai-style burger that regulars dream about between visits. The vivacious owner-operator counts Ryan Gosling and Natalie Portman among her loyal, mostly *farang* (non-Thai) customers. Look for the wall of fame near the bathrooms. (☎323-667-9809; jitladala.com; 5233 W Sunset Blvd; mains $11-30; ⊙lunch & dinner; [P])

Providence NEW AMERICAN $$$

15 Map p26, D5

Blinged out with two Michelin stars, this has long been one of LA's finest. Dishes include scallop tartare, veal sweetbreads and a lobster with roasted porcini mushrooms and spiced hazelnuts. To truly sample the goods, splurge for the nine-course tasting menu. (☎323-460-4170; www. providencela.com; 5955 Melrose Ave; mains $40-49; ⊙noon-2pm Fri, 6-10pm Mon-Fri, 5:30-10pm Sat, to 9:30pm Sun; [P])

Little Fork NEW SOUTHERN $$$

16 Map p26, D3

A converted studio, the stucco exterior is a horror show, but inside is all dark and moody, with a kitchen that churns out plates of house-smoked trout, brick-roasted chicken, a 1lb lobster roll and potato gnocchi cooked in bacon lard, tarragon and cream. (☎323-465-3675; www.littleforkla.com; 1600 Wilcox Ave; mains $9-28; ⊙11am-3pm Sat & Sun, 5-10pm Sun-Thu, to midnight Fri & Sat; [P])

Pikey GASTROPUB $$

17 Map p26, A3

This tasteful kitchen began life as Coach & Horses, one of Hollywood's favorite dives, before it was re-imagined into a place where you can get broccoli roasted with bacon, arctic char crudo with grapefruit and jalapeños, seared squid with curried chickpeas, and a slow roasted duck leg. The cocktails rock. (☎323-850-5400; www.thepikeyla.com; 7617 W Sunset Blvd; mains $12-28; ⊙noon-2am Mon-Fri, from 11am Sat & Sun)

Local Life

Hollywood Farmers Markets

LA's farmers markets supply artisanal kitchens and nourish families across the city. Hollywood has two of the best.

The Hollywood Farmers Market is very much a culinary sprawl with specialty produce from over 90 farmers and over 30 savory prepared-food stalls.

Yamashiro Farmers Market (Map p26, B2; www.yamashirorestaurant.com; 1999 N Sycamore Ave; ⏲5-9pm Thu May-Sep; Ⓟ) is really more about the views from Yamashiro's spectacular perch. Gourmet food stalls serve up delights such as miso cod tacos, grilled bratwurst and Bulgarian gelato. There's a wine-tasting bar and live music, too.

Square One   DINER $$

18 Map p26, H4

In the shadows of the sprawling Scientology campus, you'll find this adorable breakfast and lunch spot where they braise mustard and collard greens to serve with baked eggs and grits. Tacos are filled with scrambled eggs, jalapeños and chorizo, and they serve a range of gourmet salads and sandwiches too. (☑323-661-1109; www.squareonedining.com; 4854 Fountain Ave; mains $9-14; ⏲8:30am-3pm)

Oaks Gourmet   DELI $

19 Map p26, F2

A hipster deli and wine shop with a devoted following, its ultimate BLT combines heirloom tomato, creamy Camembert cheese, avocado and black-forest bacon on toasted sourdough, and specialty nights feature grilled sausages, grilled cheese and tacos. Their breakfast burrito is special. (☑323-871-8894; www.theoaksgourmet.com; 1915 N Bronson Ave; mains $8.95-11.95; ⏲7am-midnight; Ⓟ)

Hollywood Farmers Market   MARKET $

20 Map p26, D3

On the shortlist for the city's best farmers market. This Sunday-morning culinary sprawl offers organic and specialty produce vendors selling tasty prepared food, from smoothies to tamales to crepes to grilled sausages. It's a great event for the family. (www.farmernet.com; cnr Ivar & Selma Ave; ⏲8am-1pm Sun;)

Life Food Organic   RAW $

21 Map p26, D3

This place serves the healthiest fast food around. Have a chocolate shake made with almond milk, a veggie chili burger with a sesame seaweed salad on the side, and a chocolate cream pie for dessert. None of it cooked! You can dine in, but most take it away. (www.lifefoodorganic.com; 1507 N Cahuenga Ave; mains $4-14; ⏲7:30am-9pm)

Loteria Grill (p31)

Ganda
THAI **$**

Get a whiff of real Thai street food, close to Bhan Kanom Thai (see **46**  Map p26, H3). Its steam table has the same selection of seafood, chicken and veggie dishes that you'd find in any Bangkok night market. (5269 Hollywood Blvd; mains $6-8; ⊙11am-2am Sun-Thu, to 3am Sat & Sun; P)

Drinking

No Vacancy
BAR

22 Map p26, D3

An old, shingled Victorian has been converted into LA's hottest night out. Even the entrance is theatrical: you'll follow a rickety staircase into a narrow hall and enter the room of a would-be madame dressed in fishnet, who will soon press a button to reveal another staircase down into the living room and out into a courtyard. (323-465-1902; www.novacancyla.com; 1727 N Hudson Ave; ⊙8pm-2am)

La Descarga
LOUNGE

23 Map p26, G4

This tastefully frayed, sublimely sweaty rum-and-cigar lounge is a revelation. Behind the marble bar are over 100 types of rum from Haiti, Guyana, Guatemala and Venezuela. (323-466-1324; www.ladescargala.com; 1159 N Western Ave; ⊙8pm-2am Wed-Sat)

Local Life

Musso & Frank Grill

Hollywood history hangs thick in the air at **Musso & Frank Grill** (Map p26, C3; www.mussoandfrankgrill.com; 6667 Hollywood Blvd).

Charlie Chaplin used to slam gimlets at the bar and Raymond Chandler penned scripts in the high-backed booths. Word is, Mick Jagger remains a fan of the noir ambience, gentlemen bartenders and icy martinis served in small stems.

Dirty Laundry   BAR

24 Map p26, D3

Under a cotton-candy-pink apartment block of no particular import is a funky den of musty odor and great times, low ceilings, exposed pipes, good whiskey, groovy funk on the turntables and plenty of pretty people with low inhibitions. There are velvet-rope politics at work here, so reserve a table to make sure you slip through. (☎323-462-6531; dirtylaundrybarla.com; 1725 N Hudson Ave; ⏲10pm-2am)

Good Times at Davey Wayne's   BAR

25 Map p26, E3

Enter a faux garage stocked with vintage items for sale, walk through the refrigerator door and emerge in a wood-panelled, soft-rocking ode to 1970s Californication. Craft beer on tap, superb cocktails and there's even a barbecue and a bar (housed in a camper) on the deck out back. Happy hour begins here. (www.goodtimesatdavey waynes.com; 1611 N El Centro Ave; ⏲5pm-2am Mon-Fri, from 2pm Sat & Sun)

Sayers Club   CLUB

26 Map p26, D3

When rock royalty such as Prince, established stars such as the Black Keys, and even movie stars such as Joseph Gordon-Levitt decide to play secret shows in intimate environs, they come to the back room at this brick-house Hollywood nightspot, where the booths are leather, the lighting moody and the music always satisfies. (☎323-871-8416; www.sbe.com/nightlife/lo cations/thesayersclub-hollywood; 1645 Wilcox Ave; cover varies; ⏲8pm-2am Tue, Thu & Fri)

Emerson Theatre   CLUB

27 Map p26, B3

A mash-up of prohibition cocktails, scantily clad burlesque dancers, hip-hop, velvet ropes and VIP sections. The pretty people who enjoy their LA glitz party here. (☎323-525-2453; www. sbe.com/nightlife/brands/emersontheatre; 7080 Hollywood Blvd)

Cat & Fiddle   PUB

28 Map p26, D4

Morrissey to Frodo, you never know who might be popping by for Boddingtons, Sunday-night jazz or Tuesday-night trivia. Fortunately, this Brit pub staple with leafy beer garden is more about friends and conversation than faux hawks and working the deal. (www.thecatandfiddle.com; 6530 W Sunset Blvd; ⏰11:30am-2am)

Harvard & Stone BAR

29 Map p26, H3

The thing here is craft whiskey, bourbon and cocktail specials that rotate daily. It lures hipsters with live bands, burlesque troops and solid DJs. Especially on Sunday where a rockabilly theme and the sexy crowd will make you certainly twist and possibly shout. (www.harvardandstone.com; 5221 Hollywood Blvd; ⏰8pm-2am)

Javista CAFE

30 Map p26, C3

Easily the coolest coffee joint in this stretch of Hollywood. Here you'll find hipsters with lap dogs and slackers sipping organic tea and leaden coffee to keep the blood pumping. The pastries are tasty, too. (www.javistacafe.com; 6707 Sunset Blvd; ⏰7am-8pm Mon-Sat, to 7pm Sun; 📶)

Real Raw Live JUICE BAR

31 Map p26, F2

OK, we agree that there are far too many juice bars in LA these days, but we'd like this one to stick around. Here, all the slimming, toning, invigorating superfoods (such as maca, goji berries, hemp protein etc) are combined and blended into tasty concoctions. They can even set you up with a multi-day juice cleanse.

(☎323-461-4545; www.realrawlive.com; 5913 Franklin Ave; elixir shots from $4, juices from $8; ⏰8am-9pm)

Entertainment

Upright Citizens Brigade Theatre COMEDY

32 ⭐ Map p26, F2

Founded in New York by *SNL* alums Amy Poehler and Ian Roberts along with Matt Besser and Matt Walsh, this sketch-comedy group cloned itself in Hollywood in 2005 and is arguably the best improv theater in town. Most shows are $5 or $8, but Sunday's 'Asssscat' is freeeee. (☎323-908-8702; www.losangeles.ucbtheatre.com; 5919 Franklin Ave; tickets $5-10)

Fonda Theatre CONCERT VENUE

33 ⭐ Map p26, E3

The old Henry Fonda Theatre has been restored, and remains one of Hollywood's best venues for live music. It's an intimate, general-admission space with an open dance floor and balcony seating. It books progressive rock bands (think Mumford & Sons and Broken Bells), groove masters like Chromeo and can lure all-time greats like Tom Petty for intimate residencies. (☎323-464-6269; www.fondatheatre.com; 6126 Hollywood Blvd)

Pantages Theater THEATER

34 ⭐ Map p26, E3

The splendidly restored Pantages Theater is an art deco survivor from the golden age and a fabulous place to catch a play or Broadway musical. Oscars were handed out here between 1949 and 1959, when Howard Hughes owned the building. The uber noir Frolic Room bar next door was featured in *LA Confidential*. Recent shows include *Book of Mormon*. (www.pantages-theater.com; 6233 Hollywood Blvd)

Arclight Cinemas CINEMA

35 ⭐ Map p26, D4

Assigned seats and exceptional celeb sighting potential make this 14-screen multiplex the best around. If your taste dovetails with its schedule, the awesome 1963 geodesic Cinerama Dome is a must. Bonuses: age 21-plus screenings where you can booze it up, and Q&As with directors, writers and actors. Parking is $3 for four hours. (☎323-464-1478; www.arclightcinemas.com; 6360 W Sunset Blvd; tickets $14-16)

El Floridita CLUB

36 ⭐ Map p26, E4

The place for grown-up *salseros*. Order a mojito and watch the beautiful dancers do their thing (or join in if you feel you've got the moves). The Monday night jams led by Johnny Polanco y su Orquesta Amistad are legendary; make reservations at least a week in advance. (☎323-871-8612; www.elfloridita.com; 1253 N Vine St; cover $10, with dinner free; ⊙Mon, Wed, Fri & Sat)

Bardot CLUB

37 ⭐ Map p26, E3

On Monday Nights, KCRW's Chris Douridas brings **School Night** (www.itsaschoolnight.com), a free live-music club featuring buzz-worthy talent, to the atmospheric top floor of the old Avalon theater. There is no exclusivity here, but you do have to RSVP and show up early enough to get in prior to max capacity. (www.bardothollywood.com; 1735 N Vine St; ⊙Mon-Sat)

American Cinematheque CINEMA

38 ⭐ Map p26, C3

A nonprofit screening tributes, retrospectives and foreign films in the Egyptian Theatre. Directors, screen-writers and actors often swing by for post show Q&As. (www.american cinematheque.com; 6712 Hollywood Blvd; adult/senior & student $11/9)

Ford Amphitheatre CONCERT VENUE

39 ⭐ Map p26, D1

Every seat is within 100ft of the stage at this up-close-and-personal outdoor amphitheater. With the Hollywood Hills as a backdrop, catch indie bands, foreign movies and dance troupes from June to October. Picnics welcome. (☎323-461-3673; www.fordamphitheatre.com; 2580 Cahuenga Blvd E; admission $5-45; ⊙May-Oct)

Arclight Cinemas

Hotel Cafe   LIVE MUSIC

40 Map p26, D3

An anomaly on glittery Cahuenga Corridor, this intimate venue is the place for handmade music by message-minded singer-songwriters. Big names like Suzanne Vega show up on occasion but mostly it's a stepping stone for newbie balladeers. Get there early and enter from the alley. (☑323-461-2040; www.hotelcafe.com; 1623 N Cahuenga Blvd; tickets $10-20)

Improv Olympic West   COMEDY

41 Map p26, D3

Second only to the Upright Citizens Brigade in the frequency and quality of shows. It has at least three daily, starting on the hour. The Armando Show ($5) on Monday nights is hosted by a celebrity guest with suggestions from the audience. (http://west.ioimprov. com; 6366 Hollywood Blvd; admission $5-10; ☺8-11pm)

Catalina Bar & Grill   JAZZ

42 Map p26, C3

LA's premier jazz club is now tucked in an office building (enter through the garage), but once inside all is forgiven. Expect top talent such as Barbara Morrison, Kenny Burrell and Chick Corea. Two shows (almost) nightly; times vary. (☑323-466-2210; www.catalinajazzclub.com; 6725 W Sunset Blvd; cover $15-40 plus dinner or two drinks)

El Capitan Theatre

CINEMA

43 ⭐ Map p26, C3

Disney rolls out family-friendly block-busters at this movie palace, often with costumed characters putting on the Ritz in live pre-show routines. The best seats are on the balcony in the middle of the front row. VIP tickets allow you to reserve a seat and include popcorn and a beverage.
(☏800-347-6396; elcapitan.go.com; 6838 Hollywood Blvd; general admission adult/senior & child $15/12; ⛄)

Shopping

Amoeba Music

MUSIC

44 🔒 Map p26, D4

When a record store not only survives but thrives in this techno age, you know they're doing something right. Flip through half-a-million new and used CDs, DVDs, videos and vinyl at this granddaddy of music stores. Handy listening stations and its outstanding *Music We Like* booklet keep you from buying lemons. Name bands perform live in-store regularly.
(☏323-245-6400; www.amoeba.com; 6400 W Sunset Blvd; ⏰10:30am-11pm Mon-Sat, 11am-9pm Sun)

Mush

GIFTS

45 🔒 Map p26, G3

An inspiring gift, antique and home-decor boutique filled with color (dig those resin lanterns), style (you'll love the silver jewelry and mod furniture) and soul (stone Buddha anyone?). The music and the owner-operator are warm and groovy. (www.m-u-s-h.com; 5651 Hollywood Blvd; ⏰11am-6pm Tue-Sun)

Bhan Kanom Thai

THAI SWEETS

46 🔒 Map p26, H3

This is a remarkable sweet shop with all manner of Thai desserts including candy, dried fruit, gummies, sours, crisps and cakes. (www.bhankanomthai.com; 5271 Hollywood Blvd; ⏰10am-2am)

Counterpoint

MUSIC & BOOKS

At Counterpoint, situated near the Upright Citizens Brigade Theater (see 32 ⭐ Map p26, F2), woodblock stacks are packed high with used fiction, while crude plywood bins are stuffed with soul, classical and jazz vinyl. The real gems (the rare first editions and vintage rock posters) are in the collectible wing next door. (www.counterpointrecordsandbooks.com; 5911 Franklin Ave; ⏰11am-11pm)

Space 1520

MALL

47 🔒 Map p26, D3

The hippest mini-mall in Hollywood, this designer construct of brick, wood, concrete and glass is home to classic and trend-setting mini-chains like Umami Burger, Hennesy & Ingalls and Free People. (www.space1520.com; 1520 N Cahuenga Blvd; ⏰11am-9pm Mon-Fri, 10am-10pm Sat, to 9pm Sun)

Interior of Amoeba Music

Frederick's of Hollywood
LINGERIE

This famous purveyor gave us the cleavage-enhancing push-up bra and the G-string but, in 2005, competition forced it to abandon its original flagship store and move down the street to Hollywood & Highland (see 9 Map p26, C3). The new, smaller branch still sells everything from chemises to crotchless panties, all tastefully displayed with no need to blush. (www.fredericks.com; 6751 Hollywood Blvd; 10am-9pm Mon-Sat, 11am-7pm Sun)

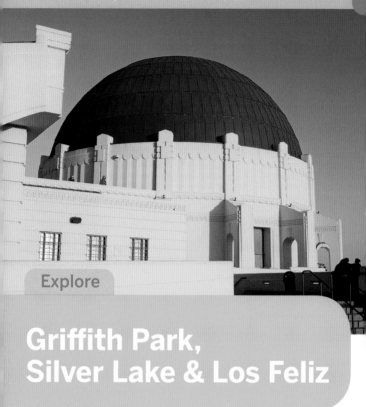

Explore

Griffith Park, Silver Lake & Los Feliz

Los Feliz, founded by mining mogul Griffith J Griffith, is one of LA's oldest, most affluent neighborhoods. *Swingers* spotlit its hipster haunts (and traits) in the mid '90s, when high rents chased up-and-comers to Silver Lake's revitalized modernist homes, boho bistros and bars. But for for all the history and palpable urban cool, the highlight here remains the 4210-acre Griffith Park.

The Sights in a Day

☀ Take your breakfast at **Alcove** (p48), alongside hipsters, yuppies and the occasional local celeb, then spend the rest of the morning breezing through boutiques and thrift shops on Hillhurst and Vermont – don't miss **Spitfire Girl** (p51) or **Skylight Books** (p50). Then check out Frank Lloyd Wright's masterful **Hollyhock House** (p46).

☀ Grab lunch at **Forage** (p48) in Silver Lake, before exploring the bohemian boutiques that define the area, such as **Matrushka Construction** (p50). Then double back to **Griffith Park** (p47) and spend the late afternoon and early evening exploring the **Griffith Observatory** (pictured left; p42) and enjoying some of the city's most magnificent views.

☾ If it's a clear, dark night, linger along the lawns around the Observatory and peer into telescopes toward heavenly bodies. Then join the crowds gabbing and grubbing at **L&E Oyster Bar** (p46) or **Thirsty Crow** (p49) for late-night drinks. Or if your timing is impeccable, ditch the cocktails and see a show at the **Greek Theatre** (p50).

 Top Sights

Griffith Observatory & Hollywood Sign (p42)

💜 **Best of Los Angeles**

Eating
Elf Cafe (p47)

Forage (p48)

Drinking
Short Stop (p49)

Thirsty Crow (p49)

Shopping
Spitfire Girl (p51)

Wacko (p51)

Getting There

Ⓜ **Metro** The area is well connected to Hollywood, Downtown and Universal City by the Metro Red Line.

Ⓜ **Metro** The most centrally located Red Line stop is Vermont/Sunset.

🚌 **Bus** MTA, LA's principal transit authority, connects Los Feliz and Silver Lake with all other parts of town. The LADOT Observatory Shuttle operates on weekends.

Top Sights
Griffith Observatory & Hollywood Sign

Two world-famous landmarks loom from either end of Griffith Park in the Hollywood Hills. The 1935 Griffith Observatory opens a window onto the universe from its perch on the southern slopes of Mt Hollywood. LA's most famous landmark is just west of the park, and first appeared in 1923 as an advertising gimmick for a real-estate development called 'Hollywoodland.' The last four letters were lopped off in the '40s. Alice Cooper and Hugh Hefner joined forces with fans to save the famous symbol in the 1970s.

◉ Map p44, B4, A2

☎ 213-473-0800

www.griffithobservatory.org

2800 E Observatory Rd

admission to observatory free

🕑 noon-10pm Tue-Fri, from 10am Sat & Sun

Griffith Observatory

Don't Miss

Samuel Oschin Planetarium

Featuring a state-of-the-art star projector and laser projection systems, and one of the largest planetarium domes in the world, the observatory's planetarium shows (adult/child under 12 yr $7/3) are one of the biggest draws. Shows bounce from the origins of the universe and our place within it, to the search for water in the solar system, to an exploration of Viking cosmology featuring a Northern Lights display that will blow your mind.

Rooftop Vistas

Head to the roof to peek through the refracting and solar telescopes housed in the smaller domes. The sweeping views of the Hollywood Hills and the gleaming city below are just as spectacular, especially at sunset.

Hollyridge Trail

OK, so you desperately, compulsively, must hike to the Hollywood Sign where in 1932 a struggling young actress named Peggy Entwistle leapt her way into local lore (and her own death) from the letter 'H.' Take Beachwood Dr from Franklin until its end at the Hollyridge Trailhead. Follow the trail (don't worry, there are signs), make a left at the first fork and a right at the second fork. Expect spectacular views along the way. You'll wind up below the letters, which are fenced off to preserve them from would-be vandals. Bring plenty of water. The hike takes about an hour one way.

☑ Top Tips

▶ It helps to have a car to explore Griffith Park, but you can access the observatory via public transport on weekends (10am to 10pm). Take the Metro to Vermont/Sunset and hop on the LADOT shuttle (25¢, 35 minutes) from there.

▶ Stay after dark to peer into the Zeist Telescope on the roof or staff wheel additional telescopes out to the front lawn if you can't be bothered to wait in line.

▶ If you'd rather not hike up to the fenced-off letters themselves, good viewing spots include from Hollywood & Highland, the top of Beachwood Dr and the Griffith Observatory.

✕ Take a Break

Both the Hollyridge Trail and Griffith Observatory lawn demand a picnic, and there's no better place to stock up than the **Oaks Gourmet** (☎323-871-8894; www.theoaksgourmet.com; 1915 N Bronson Ave; ⏰7am-midnight; P), a five-minute drive away.

W Colorado Blvd

W Broadway

1 km
0.5 miles

Glendale Water
Reclamation
Plant

Los Angeles River

Golden State Fwy

Los Feliz Blvd

North
Atwater
Park

Los Feliz Blvd

Autry
National
Center

Wilson
Golf
Course

Crystal Springs Dr

Vista del Valle Dr

Commonweal
Ave

N Vermont Ave

Los Angeles Zoo &
Botanical Gardens

Harding
Golf
Course

Griffith Park

Mt Bell
(1587ft)

Mt Hollywood
(1625ft)

Mt Hollywood Dr

Vermont
Canyon Rd

Roosevelt
Municipal Golf
Course

21

Mt Chapel
(1612ft)

Mulholland
Hwy

Griffith
Observatory

Griffith Park Dr

Brush
Canyon

Western
Canyon Dr

Canyon Dr

Forest Lawn
Memorial Park
& Hollywood Hills

Sennet
Canyon

Mt Lee Dr

Mt Lee
(1640ft)

Hollywood
Sign

N Beachwood
Dr

Silver Lake Reservoir

Riverside Dr

Rowena Ave

26 ▣

MichELTORENA St

SILVER LAKE

Griffith Park Blvd

Hyperion Ave

Silver Lake Blvd

5 ▣

Micheltorena St

N Benton Way

Reservoir St

16 ▶
6 ⊗

W Sunset Blvd

Marathon St

18 ▣

Silver Lake Blvd

22 ▶

Effie St

12 ⊗
19 ⊗

Edgecliff Dr
Lucile Ave

15 ⊗

Bellevue Recreation Center

Marathon St

N Hoover St

St George St

John Marshall High School

4 ⊙

Sunset Dr

14 ⊗
7 ⊗

Myra Ave
Sanborn Ave
Hyperion Ave

N Hoover St

Clayton Ave

N Virgil Ave

17 ▣

Burns Ave

Monroe St

Hollywood Fwy

9 ⊗⊗
11 ⊗

Hillhurst Ave

24 ▣
8 ⊗
13 ⊗

Russell Ave
Melbourne Ave
Kingswell Ave
Prospect Ave

Hollywood Blvd

10 ⊗

23 ▣
25 ▣

Vermont/
Sunset Ⓜ

LOS FELIZ

20 ▣

N Vermont Ave

Finley Ave

Franklin Ave

Barnsdall Art Park 1 ⊙

Hollyhock House

Lexington Ave

Los Angeles City College

Vermont/Santa Monica/LACC Ⓜ

Hollywood/
Western Ⓜ

W Sunset Blvd

Fountain Ave

Romaine St

Santa Monica Blvd

N Western Ave

Beverly Blvd

Melrose Ave

Hollywood Fwy

Los Feliz Blvd

Hollywood Blvd

Franklin Ave

Hollywood Fwy

N Bronson Ave

Hollywood Forever Cemetery

Beth Olam Memorial Park

For reviews see	
⊙ Top Sights	p42
⊙ Sights	p46
⊗ Eating	p46
⊗ Drinking	p49
⊗ Entertainment	p50
▣ Shopping	p50

A B C D E

5

6

7

8

Sights

Hollyhock House
LANDMARK

1 ◉ Map p44, C6

Oil heiress Aline Barnsdall commissioned Frank Lloyd Wright to design this hilltop home in 1919. However, the project ended sourly and was finished by architect Rudolph Schindler. Due to Wright's Romanza-style design there's an easy flow between rooms and courtyards. Note abstract imagery of the hollyhock, Aline's preferred flower, throughout. (☎323-644-6269; www.hollyhockhouse.net; 4800 Hollywood Blvd; adult/student/child $7/3/free; ⊘tours hourly 12:30-3:30pm Wed-Sun; P)

Los Angeles Zoo & Botanical Gardens
ZOO

2 ◉ Map p44, D1

The zoo, with its 1100 finned, feathered and furry friends from over 250 species, rarely fails to enthrall the little ones. What began in 1912 as a refuge for retired circus animals now brings in over a million visitors each year. (☎323-644-4200; www.lazoo.org; 5333 Zoo Dr; adult/senior/child $18/15/13; ⊘10am-5pm, closed Christmas; P🚼)

Autry National Center
MUSEUM

3 ◉ Map p44, D1

Want to know how the West was really won? Then mosey over to this excellent museum – its exhibits on the good, the bad and the ugly of America's westward expansion rope in even the most reluctant cowpokes. Kids can pan for gold and explore a stagecoach. Year-round gallery talks, symposia, film screenings and other cultural events spur the intellect. (☎323-667-2000; www.autrynationalcenter.org; 4700 Western Heritage Way; adult/seniors & students/child $10/6/4, 2nd Tue each month free; ⊘10am-4pm Tue-Fri, to 5pm Sat & Sun; P)

John Marshall High School
NOTABLE BUILDING

4 ◉ Map p44, D5

A 1931 historic brick-and-stone beauty with peaked windows, exterior moldings and a fantastic athletic field visible from the street. Leo – you know the one – suffered through high school here. (www.johnmarshallhs.org; 3939 Tracy St)

Eating

L&E Oyster Bar
SEAFOOD $$$

5 🍴 Map p44, E7

Silver Lake's seafood house opened to rave reviews in 2012 and is still a neighborhood darling. Locals and celebs claim tables in the intimate dining room and heated porch to feast on raw and grilled oysters, smoked mussels and whole roasted fish dressed in miso, pickled ginger, chili and garlic. There's a raw bar upstairs. (☎323-660-2255; www.leoysterbar.com; 1637 Silver Lake Blvd; mains $17-28; ⊘5-10pm Mon-Thu, to 11pm Fri & Sat)

Hollyhock House

Elf Cafe
VEGETARIAN $$

6 Map p44, E8

One of the best – if not the very best – vegetarian (not vegan) restaurants in LA. Start with feta wrapped in grape leaves and some spiced olives and almonds, then a kale salad dressed with citrus, wild mushroom risotto and a fantastic kebab of seared oyster mushrooms. (☎213-484-6829; www.elfcafe. com; 2135 Sunset Blvd; mains $12-20)

Café Stella
FRENCH $$$

7 Map p44, D7

As charming as it gets, here is a cloud of clinking glasses, red wine, good jazz and classic French bistro cuisine under a tented patio and rambling

Local Life

Griffith Park
A gift to the city in 1896 by mining mogul Griffith J Griffith, **Griffith Park** (☎323-913-4688; www.laparks. org/dos/parks/griffithpk; 4730 Crystal Springs Dr; admission free; ☉5am-10:30pm, trails sunrise-sunset; P 🛝) is LA's playground with facilities for all age levels and interests. At five times the size of New York's Central Park, it is one of the country's largest urban green spaces, and its 53 miles of hiking trails are the domain of local families whenever the sun shines. Stop by the ranger's office for a map and list of attractions.

into an antiquated dining room. Artful and inviting, it bustles at lunch and is packed for dinner. (☎323-666-0265; www.cafestella.com; 3932 W Sunset Blvd; mains $10-36; ◷9am-3pm & 6-11pm Tue-Sat, to 10pm Sun; Ⓟ)

Alcove   CAFE $$

8 Map p44, C5

Hillhurst's choice breakfast hangout, this sunny cafe spills onto a multilevel, streetside brick patio. It's housed in a restored 1897 Spanish-style duplex, and the food is quite good. There's crab-cake Benedict, bison chili omelettes, and crepes stuffed with espresso-infused cream. (☎323-644-0100; www.thealcovecafe.com; 1929 Hillhurst Ave; mains $10-17; ◷6am-midnight; Ⓟ🚻)

Little Dom's   ITALIAN $$

9 Map p44, C5

An understated yet stylish Italian deli and restaurant with deep booths, marble tables and wood floors. It does a dynamite kale salad and good thin-crust pizza. But it's beloved for its anti-pasti and sandwiches – especially the fried oyster po'boy. If you don't want full service, pop into its deli next door. (☎323-661-0055; www.littledoms.com; 2128 Hillhurst Ave; pizza $11, mains $15-41; ◷8am-3pm & 5:30-11pm Mon-Thu, to midnight Fri, 8am-midnight Sat, to 11pm Sun; Ⓟ)

Ramekin   DESSERTS $

10 Map p44, C6

A sweet addition to Vermont Ave, Ramekin specializes in made-to-order

desserts such as pumpkin cheesecake, persimmon tarts, passion-fruit panna cotta, berry cobbler, chocolate bread pudding and strawberry brick toast. They also offer homemade ice creams and some tasty sandwiches, if you're in a savory mood. (☎323-667-9627; www.ramekinla.com; 1726 N Vermont Ave; dishes $5-8)

Mess Hall   GASTROPUB $$

11 Map p44, C5

Formerly The Derby, a swing dance spot made famous by the film *Swingers*, it is now a gastropub where you'll find $1 oysters and $5 beers on Tuesdays. It's been written up for having one of the best burgers in LA, and they also do a pulled-pork sandwich and a kale Caesar. (☎323-660-6377; www.messhallkitchen.com; 4500 Los Feliz Blvd; mains $15-31; ◷11:30am-3pm & 4-11pm Mon-Thu, to midnight Fri, 10am-3pm & 5pm-midnight Sat, 10am-3pm & 4-11pm Sun)

Forage   MARKET, CAFE $$

12 Map p44, D7

Ignore the somewhat soulless design and pair a protein (*jidori* chicken or flank steak) with a couple of gourmet deli salads. Or just nibble on a quiche or crostini. It's all delicious here. Hence the packed house. (www.foragela.com; 3823 W Sunset Blvd; mains $7-13; ◷lunch & dinner Tue-Sat; 🚌MTA 2)

Yuca's   MEXICAN $

13 Map p44, C5

Location, location, location…is definitely not what lures people to this parking-lot snack shack. It's the tacos, stupid! And the *tortas,* burritos and other Mexi faves that earned the Herrera family the coveted James Beard Award in 2005. (☎323-662-1214; www.yucasla.com; 2056 Hillhurst Ave; items $4-10; ⏰11am-6pm Mon-Sat)

Blossom

VIETNAMESE $$

14 Map p44, D7

The Silver Lake edition of the Downtown favorite, Blossom serves *pho* with your choice of rare steak, brisket, tendon, tripe, chicken, shrimp or tofu. They also simmer a handful of curries and stir-fry vermicelli noodles. Seafood lovers should consider the crab noodle soup: dungeness crab and Manila clams, eggs, vermicelli noodles and red cabbage in tomato broth. (☎323-953-8345; www.blossomrestaurant.com; 4019 W Sunset Blvd; mains $9-12; ⏰noon-4pm & 5:30-11pm; 📶)

Heywood

SANDWICHES $$

15 Map p44, D7

If you enjoy that good ol' American staple, the grilled cheese sandwich, then stop at this popular concrete-floor cafe where they do 'em all gourmet like. Try the house special, Heywood: it comes with aged English cheddar and caramelized onion confit on fresh sourdough. Bonus fact: they stay open until 3am on party nights! (www.heywoodgrilledcheese.com; 3337 W Sunset Blvd; sandwiches $10-12; ⏰11am-10pm Sun-Wed, to 3am Thu-Sat)

Drinking

Short Stop

CLUB

16 Map p44, E8

Echo Park's beloved and deceptively sprawling dive has a dance floor in one room, a bar strobing ballgames on flat screens in another, and a pool table and pinball machines in still another section. Longtime Echo Park locals and new breed hipsters bump shoulders and more here, especially on Motown Mondays when vintage jams fill the room with joy. (☎213-482-4942; 1455 W Sunset Blvd; ⏰5pm-2am Mon-Fri, from 2pm Sat & Sun)

Virgil

BAR

17 Map p44, C7

A local joint serving craft cocktails. A stocked calendar of entertainment from live comedy to bands and DJs takes it from feeling like a neighborhood spot early in the evening to something wilder late at night. (www.thevirgil.com; 4519 Santa Monica Blvd; ⏰7pm-close)

Thirsty Crow

BAR

18 Map p44, D8

A loving ode to the fiery sweetness that is a classic small-batch Kentucky bourbon (it has more than 60 kinds). Yes, the bartenders can mix and muddle fresh craft cocktails, but, puleeeze, do Uncle Jessup proud and sip yours neat. It has live music every Sunday. (www.thirstycrowbar.com; 2939 W Sunset Blvd; ⏰5pm-2am Mon-Sat, 2pm-2am Sun)

Good

MICROBREW

19 Map p44, D7

Think: 500 microbrews from California, Belgium, Brazil, the Czech Republic. It serves flights, table-side draft towers and on Wednesday it's Mystery Beer Night when the bartender will pour the beer of his choosing for just $3. (www.goodmicrobrew.com; 3725 W Sunset Blvd; 11am-10pm Mon-Thu, to 11pm Fri, 9am-11pm Sat, to 10pm Sun)

Bru

CAFE

20 Map p44, C5

Los Feliz's uber-cool coffee bar comes with exposed rafters, rotating local art on the walls, and a marble slab common table where locals camp out, suck down coffee and tap their feet to indie rock. (323-664-7500; www.brucoffeebar.com; 1866 N Vermont Ave; coffee drinks $3-5; 7am-8pm Mon-Sat, from 8am Sun;)

Entertainment

Greek Theatre

CONCERT VENUE

21 Map p44, C4

A more intimate version of the Hollywood Bowl, this 5800-seat outdoor amphitheater tucked into a wooded hillside of Griffith Park is much beloved for its vibe and variety, featuring acts from Los Lobos to MGMT to Willie Nelson. Parking is stacked, so plan on a post-show wait. (323-665-5857; www.greektheatrela.com; 2700 N Vermont Ave; May-Oct)

Bootleg Theater

ARTS VENUE

22 Map p44, D8

Part progressive-rock and folk venue, part theater space, part multidisciplinary arts foundation and laboratory. This restored 1930s warehouse hosts one-off shows and long-term residencies for edgy indie bands and up and comers. It also supports spoken word, dance and dramatic artists pushing boundaries. (www.bootlegtheater.org; 2220 Beverly Blvd)

Shopping

Skylight Books

BOOKS

23 Map p44, C5

Like so many moths, bookworms are drawn to this skylight: a loft-like indie bookstore focusing on local, non-traditional and foreign authors. It also hosts several book groups and runs meet-the-author events. (323-660-1175; www.skylightbooks.com; 1818 N Vermont Ave; 10am-10pm)

Matrushka Construction

FASHION

Who says fashion has to be superficial? Lara Howe crafts her sublime, tailored designs from remnant fabrics personally and locally sourced by the owner-operator. The fabrics are still top notch, but are simply either vintage or discarded by large corporate manufacturers. It's close to Forage Cafe (see

12 Map p44, D7; www.matrushka.com; 3822 W Sunset Blvd)

Wacko store

Spitfire Girl

GIFTS

24 Map p44, C5

One of our favorite gift boutiques in the Southland trades in a take on quirk. Expect gift and photography books, its own stuffed-gnome and throw-pillow line (that's how the business launched), and organic and aromatic candles and soaps. (www.spitfiregirl.com; 1939 Hillhurst Ave)

Wacko

COLLECTIBLES

25 Map p44, C6

Billy Shire's giftorium of camp and kitsch has been a fun browse for over three decades. Pick up a dashboard Jesus or a Frida Kahlo mesh bag. It has a great selection of comics, books by California authors like Ray Bradbury and Philip K Dick, and in back is La Luz de Jesus, one of LA's top lowbrow art galleries. (☎323-663-0122; www.soap plant.com; 4633 Hollywood Blvd; ☺11am-7pm Mon-Wed, to 9pm Thu-Sat, noon-6pm Sun)

Broome Street General Store

BOUTIQUE

26 Map p44, E5

Locals love this cozy boutique-cum-cafe set in a converted house for its generous, leafy front patio, designer denim, wool sweaters and upmarket organic beauty products. And caffeine. Mostly they're here for caffeine. (www.broomest general.com; 2912 Rowena Ave; ☺8am-7pm Mon-Sat, 9am-5pm Sun)

Local Life
Cruising Echo Park

If you dig the uneasy interface of edgy urban art, music and culture in multi-ethnic neighborhoods, you'll love Echo Park, punctuated by the fountain lake featured in Polanski's *Chinatown*. True, the artists and hipsters have arrived, but the *panaderías* and *cevicherías* happily remain.

Getting There

🚗 Just west of Downtown, Sunset Blvd is the main thoroughfare. You may also access Echo Park from I-101.

🚌 Metro bus line 2 serves the district.

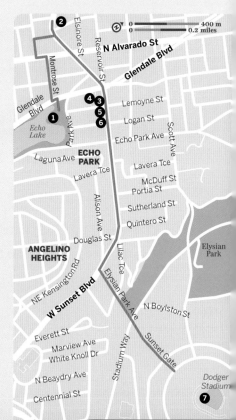

① Echo Park Lake

A former reservoir to homesteading families in the late 19th century, **Echo Park Lake** (www.laparks.org; 751 Echo Park Ave; P) is best known as the setting for Jake Gittis' surreptitious rowboating shenanigans in Polanski's classic film, and for its keyhole vistas toward downtown. Find the boathouse and rent a pedal boat or a canoe with the kids.

② I Am 8 Bit

Echo Park's funkiest art space, **I Am 8 Bit** (www.iam8bit.com; 2147 W Sunset Blvd; ⏱1-8pm Thu, to 9pm Fri, noon-9pm Sat, noon-6pm Sun) offers stellar art shows at its expansive 4500-sq-ft gallery in the heart of Echo Park.

③ Deepest Dish

Chicago deep-dish pizza is served at **Masa** (www.masaofechopark.com; 1800 W Sunset Blvd; mains $13-17; ⏱11am-11pm Mon-Thu, to midnight Fri, 8am-midnight Sat, to 11pm Sun; P) in whimsical environs that recall the wild, colorful swirl of New Orleans, right down to the swing music. They do brunch on weekends.

④ Night Music

Eastsiders hungry for an eclectic alchemy of sounds pack the **Echo** (www.attheecho.com; 1822 W Sunset Blvd; cover varies). It books indie bands like Black Rebel Motorcycle Club, and also has regular club nights in the larger Echoplex Theater.

⑤ 826 LA

At first glance, the **Time Travel Mart** (📞213-413-3388; www.826la.org; 1714 W Sunset Blvd; admission free; ⏱noon-8pm Mon-Fri, to 6pm Sat & Sun) is a convenience store for time travelers, stocked with anything a time traveler might need. But it's really just a front for a drop-in tutoring and writing program, the brainchild of McSweeney's founder and author Dave Eggers.

⑥ Kind Kreme

Sage (📞310-456-1492; www.sagevegan bistro.com; 1700 W Sunset Blvd; mains $10-14; ⏱11am-10pm Mon-Wed, to 11pm Thu & Fri, 9am-4pm & 5-11pm Sat, to 10pm Sun; 🖊♿) is an organic vegan kitchen with sandwiches and veggie burgers, crafted with love and talent and served in heaped portions. And the menu is the *second*-best thing here. The best? That would be **Kind Kreme's** (www.kindkreme. com) good-for-you, raw ice cream. Taste to believe.

⑦ Dodger Stadium

Built in 1962 and one of Major League Baseball's classic ballparks, **Dodger Stadium** (📞866-363-4377; www.dodgers. com; 1000 Elysian Park Ave; ⏱Apr-Sep) is now offering regular behind-the-scenes tours through the press box, the Dodger dugout, the Dugout Club, the field and the Tommy Lasorda Training Center. Of course, the best way to experience it is to catch a ballgame.

Explore

West Hollywood & Beverly Hills

In West Hollywood, rainbow flags fly proudly over Santa Monica Blvd and the set-piece Sunset Strip is where Hollywood has mingled for decades. Of course, ever since Will Rogers founded it, Beverly Hills has been the standard-bearer of Angelino wealth and power. And there remains ample bling on her boulevards.

The Sights in a Day

☀️ Breakfast at **Luca on Sunset** (p61), then hike **Runyon Canyon** (p58) before it gets too hot. Afterwards, meander down to Melrose Ave to enjoy a long shop that starts off high end with **Reformation** (p65) and **Nudie Jeans** (p67) and ends in that mosh pit of kitsch between Fairfax and La Brea.

☀️ Make like Larry King and grab a classic deli sandwich at **Nate'n Al** (p61) in Beverly Hills or head down the block for a Mediterranean lunch with a twist at **Momed** (p61), a stroll along **Rodeo Dr** (pictured left; p65) and a digression into **Barneys** (p67).

🌙 Begin with a cracked-ice cocktail at **Comme Ca** (p62), where the menu will likely be inviting, but if you manage to put off dinner consider a reservation at **Hakkasan** (p61) or industry haunt **Grill on the Alley** (p60). Unless you plan on catching a show at **Groundlings** (p64), after dinner make the drive to the legendary **Bar Marmont** (p62) and stay awhile.

 Best of Los Angeles

Eating
Connie & Ted's (p59)

Drinking
Bar Marmont (p62)

Comme Ca (p62)

Shopping
Barneys New York (p67)

Reformation (p65)

Fred Segal (p65)

Diane von Furstenberg (p66)

Melrose Trading Post (p67)

Getting There

🚌 **Bus** MTA, LA's principal transit authority, connects West Hollywood with all other parts of town.

0 _____ 1 km
0 _____ 0.5 miles

Greystone Park

N Doheny Dr

SUNSET STRIP

Horn Ave

W Sunset Blvd

14 ✕

★ 29

🔒 36

Holloway Dr

WEST HOLLYWOOD

Doheny Rd

Loma Vista Dr

W Sunset Blvd

Cynthia St

Palm Ave

✕ 11

West Knoll Dr

N La Cienega Blvd

Elevado Ave

N Sierra Dr

16 ✕

N Alta Dr

N Arden Dr

25 ✕ 13

Pacific Design Center

🅿

3 ◉ 🛈

21

24 🔒

N Hillcrest Rd

N Maple Dr

N Palm Dr

9 ✕ ★
31

Melrose Ave

N Elm Dr

N Foothill Rd

Beverly Gardens Park

Civic Center Dr

N Robertson Blvd

N San Vicente Dr

Huntley Dr

N La Cienega Blvd

Carmelita Ave

Santa Monica Blvd

Foothill Rd

N Elm Dr

N Maple Dr

N Palm Dr

N Oakhurst Dr

N Wetherly Dr

N Almont Dr

Alden Dr

N Sherbourne Dr

🔒 38

W 3rd St

Burton Way

18

35

N Cañon Dr

N Beverly Dr

N Rodeo Dr

N Alpine Dr

Dayton Way

Clifton Way

BEVERLY HILLS

S Wetherly Dr

S Almont Dr

S La Peer Dr

S Swall Dr

S Clark Dr

Colgate Ave

N Arnaz Dr

N Hamel Dr

N Willaman Dr

S Sherbourne Dr

S Holt Ave

S Corning St

N La Cienega Blvd

12 ✕

20 ✕ 19

2

6 ◉ Ace Gallery

17 ◉

46 🔒

Wilshire Blvd

E
23
33
F
4
G
W Sunset Blvd
H

Kings Rd
De Longpre Ave
N Detroit St
N La Brea Ave
1

William S Hart Park
28
15
Fountain Ave
N Orange Grove Ave
N Ogden Dr
N Genesee Ave
Hampton Ave
Plummer Park
N Vista St
N Martel Ave
N Fuller Ave

N Flores St
WEST HOLLYWOOD
Lexington Ave
44
Norton Ave
Norton Ave

Santa Monica Blvd
7
Santa Monica Blvd
26
2

N Kings Rd
N Sweetzer Ave
Romaine St
N Laurel Ave
N Edinburgh Ave
N Hayworth Ave
N Fairfax Ave
N Orange Grove Ave
N Ogden Dr
N Genesee Ave
N Curson Ave
N Sierra Bonita Ave
Poinsettia Recreation Center
Romaine St

Willoughby St
Willoughby Ave

Waring Ave
Waring Ave

34
45
22
10
30
3

Melrose Ave
1
Melrose Ave

37
39
8
43
41
Melrose Ave
42

BEVERLY CENTER DISTRICT
Clinton St
N Fairfax Ave
N Spaulding Ave
N Stanley Ave
N Curson Ave
Clinton St
MELROSE/ LA BREA

Rosewood Ave
N Gardner St
N Vista St
N Martel Ave
N Fuller Ave
N Poinsettia Pl
N Alta Vista Blvd
N Formosa Ave
N Detroit St
N La Brea Ave

Oakwood Ave

Beverly Blvd
FAIRFAX DISTRICT
Beverly Blvd

W 1st St
S Edinburgh Ave
MID-CITY
W 1st St
5
4

W 3rd St
The Grove
The Grove Dr
Pan Pacific Park
S Gardner St
S Vista St
S Martel Ave
S Fuller Ave
S Poinsettia Pl
S Alta Vista Blvd
Nick Metropolis
S Detroit St
S La Brea Ave

S Sweetzer Ave
Colgate Ave
S Fairfax Ave
W 3rd St
Colgate Ave
5

S Curson Ave
W 4th St

Sights

Melrose Ave
COMMERCIAL DISTRICT

1 ⊙ Map p56, G3

A popular shopping strip as famous for its epic people-watching as it is for its consumer fruits. You'll see hair (and people) of all shades and styles, and everything from Gothic jewels to custom sneakers to medical marijuana to stuffed porcupines available for a price. The strip is located between Fairfax and La Brea.

Museum of Tolerance
MUSEUM

2 ⊙ Map p56, A5

Run by the Simon Wiesenthal Center, this museum uses interactive technology to engage visitors in discussion and contemplation around racism and bigotry, with particular focus given to the Holocaust. You can study various Nazi-era memorabilia, including bunk beds from the Majdanek camp and Göring's dress-uniform cap. (ℐinfo 310-553-8403, reservations 310-772-2505; www.museumoftolerance.com; 9786 W Pico Blvd; adult/senior/student $15.50/12.50/11.50, Anne Frank Exhibit adult/senior/student $15.50/13.50/12.50; ⏰10am-6:30pm Sun-Wed, to 9:30pm Thu, 10am-5pm Fri; P)

Pacific Design Center
LANDMARK

3 ⊙ Map p56, C3

Interior design is big in WeHo, with over 120 trade-only showrooms at the Pacific Design Center and dozens more in the surrounding **Avenues of Art & Design** (Beverly Blvd, Robertson Blvd & Melrose Ave). PDC showrooms generally sell only to design pros, but often you can get items at a mark-up through the Buying Program. (www.pacificdesigncenter.com; 8687 Melrose Ave; ⏰9am-5pm Mon-Fri)

Runyon Canyon
HIKING

4 ⊙ Map p56, F1

This 130-acre public park is as famous for its beautiful, bronzed and buff runners as it is for the panoramic views from the upper ridge. Follow the wide, partially paved fire road up, then take the smaller track down the canyon where you'll pass the remains of the Runyon estate. (www.lamountains.com; 2000 N Fuller Ave; ⏰dawn-dusk)

Local Life
The Hammer

Once a vanity project of the late oil tycoon Armand Hammer, his eponymous **museum** (http://hammer.ucla.edu; 10899 Wilshire Blvd; admission free; ⏰11am-8pm Tue-Fri, to 5pm Sat & Sun) has become a widely respected art space. Selections from Hammer's personal collection include relatively minor works by Monet, Van Gogh and Mary Cassat, but the museum really shines when it comes to cutting-edge contemporary exhibits featuring local, under-represented and controversial artists. Best of all, it's free.

Nick Metropolis

ANTIQUES

5 Map p56, H4

There's nothing quite like this street corner occupied with a pack rat's extravagance. Here are any manner of decommissioned neon and street signs, collectible antique furniture and cartoon character statues – a hodgepodge of the commercial and the bizarre. (www.nickmetropolis.com; 100 S La Brea; ⏱10am-7pm Mon-Sat, from 11am Sun)

Ace Gallery

GALLERY

6 Map p56, A5

Two floors of top-level, modern, large-format art in an iconic converted bank building. Expect everything from post-modern, almost steampunk, pen-and-ink drawings from Laurie Lipton, to flat circular spirals of color and mayhem from Gary Lang. The sculpture is amazing, too. (☎310-858-9090; www.acegallery.net; 9430 Wilshire Blvd; ⏱10am-6pm Tue-Sat)

Eating

Connie & Ted's

SEAFOOD $$$

7 Map p56, F2

The design is an instant classic, and there are always up to a dozen oyster varieties at the stocked raw bar. Fresh fish is panfried or grilled to order. The lobster roll can be served cold with mayo or hot with drawn butter, and the shellfish marinara is a sacred thing. (☎323-848-2722; www.connieandteds.com;

BARRY WINIKER/GETTY IMAGES ©

Pacific Design Center

8171 Santa Monica Blvd; mains $12-26; ⏱5-11pm Mon & Tue, noon-11pm Wed-Sun)

Hart & the Hunter

SOUTHERN $$$

8 Map p56, F3

This spare, Southern-inspired kitchen with a small rotating menu is based at one of our favorite new hotels, the Pali. The shrimp and grits awash in a bacon vinaigrette is a staple at lunch and brunch, but they also serve a kale salad and smoked trout on toast; the biscuits are legit too. Book ahead. (☎323-424-3055; www.thehartandthehunter.com; 7950 Melrose Ave; mains $10-32; ⏱7am-10pm Tue-Thu, to 11pm Fri & Sat, to 9pm Sun)

Dan Tana's ITALIAN $$$

9 Map p56, B3

There are three reasons this exclusive yet somehow still laid-back, 46-year-old Italian chophouse remains packed with Hollywood celebrities and sports stars on a near nightly basis: the steaks, the service and the hours. It serves late supper until 1:30am. (☎310-275-9444; www.dantanasrestaurant.com; 9071 Santa Monica Blvd; mains $23-39; ⏰5pm-1:30am; P)

Blu Jam CAFE $$

10 Map p56, G3

Yes, it serves lunch, but you should come for the all-day breakfast with organic coffee and tea. There are two pages of mains that include four kinds of Benedict and a popular Corn Flakes–crusted 'crunchy French toast.' (www.blujamcafe.com; 7371 Melrose Ave; mains $7-15; ⏰8am-4pm; P 🖉 ♿)

Fresh Corn Grill GRILL $$

11 Map p56, D2

A fantastic, fresh, all-natural joint with affordable grilled veggie salads, semi-authentic tacos, home-baked desserts and good coffee. It's a perfect choice for quick healthy eats, and the side of grilled corn is fantastic. (☎310-855-9592; www.freshcorngrill.com; 8714 Santa Monica Blvd; mains $10-13; ⏰11:30am-10pm; 📶)

Grill on the Alley CONTINENTAL $$$

12 Map p56, A5

A back-alley marble, oak and leather steakhouse where Hollywood heavyweights – who flock here from nearby agencies – slug it out over lunch. It's known for the steak, but the grilled ahi, salmon and whitefish are divine, and they do a terrific Joe's special if you'd rather have brunch. (☎310-276-0615; www.thegrill.com; 9560 Dayton Way; mains $16-39; ⏰11:30am-9pm Mon, to 10pm Tue-Thu, to 10:30pm Fri & Sat, 5-9pm Sun)

Hamburger Habit BURGERS $

13 Map p56, C3

The greasy burgers are middling at best, but the after-sundown scene, which may include restaurant sing-alongs and topless men dancing on tables, can be wonderful, if you time it right. (☎310-659-8774; 8954 Santa Monica Blvd; mains $5-8; ⏰10am-midnight)

Night + Market THAI $$

14 Map p56, B2

Related to Talesai, a long-running Thai joint on the strip, this kitchen is dedicated to authentic Thai street food and Thai-inspired fusion (we're thinking of you, catfish tamale!). Start with the pork satay or *larb lanna* (chopped pork salad), then move onto the *tom yum*; *chiengrei* herb sausage is a winner too. (☎310-275-9724; www.nightmarketla.com; 9041 W Sunset Blvd; dishes $7-12; ⏰6-10:30pm Tue-Sun)

Luca on Sunset

CAFE **$$**

15 Map p56, F1

A fun market kitchen that's family owned and run. Luca does pastas, pizzas, roast chicken and turkey burgers and a range of salads and sandwiches, but the breakfasts are the thing. From artichoke and goat cheese scrambles to breakfast calzones to challah French toast, you will be satisfied. (☑323-822-2900; www.lucaonsunset.com; 7950 Sunset Blvd; mains $10-17; ⏱7am-midnight)

Juliano's Raw

RAW **$$**

16 Map p56, C3

Chef Juliano serves his brand of all-raw, veggie, organic cuisine (and the best smoothies on earth) which has earned him rave reviews and a spot on *Oprah*. Sit by the fountain on the patio or in the cozy, glass-box dining room. (☑310-288-0989; www.planetraw.com; 8951 Santa Monica Blvd; mains $9-25; ⏱9am-midnight)

Momed

MEDITERRANEAN **$$**

17 Map p56, A5

Yes, it has the traditional Mediterranean dishes covered, but it also melts avocado into its hummus, crafts shawarma from duck breast, oven-dried tomatoes and fig confit, and loads flat breads with shredded *jidori* chicken, Turkish apricots and spicy tomato spread. (☑310-270-4444; www.atmomed.com; 233 S Beverly Dr; mains

$5-24; ⏱11am-9:30pm Mon-Thu, to 10pm Fri, 10am-10pm Sat & Sun)

Nate'n Al

DELI **$$**

18 Map p56, A5

Dapper seniors, chatty girlfriends, busy execs and even Larry King have kept this New York–style nosh spot busy since 1945. The huge menu brims with corned beef, lox and other old-school favorites, but we're partial to the pastrami, made fresh on-site. (☑310-274-0101; www.natenal.com; 414 N Beverly Dr; dishes $6.50-13; ⏱7am-9pm;)

Bouchon

FRENCH **$$$**

19 Map p56, A5

Quiche and salad, oysters on the half-shell, mussels steamed in white-wine sauce and steak-frites, Thomas Keller's Bouchon empire brings you classic French bistro cuisine in classy but not stuffy environs. You can taste the goods at a discount at Bar Bouchon downstairs. (☑310-279-9910; www.bouchonbistro.com; 235 N Cañon Dr; mains $17-59; ⏱11:30am-9pm Mon, to 10:30pm Tue-Fri, 11am-10:30pm Sat, to 9pm Sun; P)

Hakkasan

CHINESE FUSION **$$$**

20 Map p56, A5

Beverly Hills' fancy new Chinese spot in the ground floor of the MGM Building serves wok-fried tenderloin and lobster, claypot chicken, truffle-braised noodles, and jasmine-tea smoked short rib. It's pricey but an experience. The decor, from the marble hostess bar to leather booths paired off by labyrinthine-like Chinese screens, exudes swanky sexy. ([📞]310-888-8661; www.hakkasan.com; 233 N Beverly Dr; mains $26-68; [🕐]noon-2:30pm & 5-11pm Mon-Thu, to midnight Fri & Sat)

Comme Ca
FRENCH $$$

21 [🍴] Map p56, D3

The dining is French bistro classic, served in white-leather booths as jazz wafts over you in the sleek throw-back space. The burger earns raves (though it better, for $18), and that bar... Cocktails do not get much better. ([📞]310-782-1178; www.commecarestaurant.com; 8479 Melrose Ave; mains $18-29; [🕐]6-10pm Tue-Thu, to 11pm Fri, 11am-2:30pm & 6-11pm Sat, 11am-2:30pm Sun; [P])

Local Life
Yakitoriya

An easy 15-minute drive from Beverly Hills, **Yakitoriya** ([📞]310-479-5400; 11301 W Olympic Blvd; dishes $2.50-27; [🕐]6-10:30pm Mon, Wed-Sun; [♿]) is a chef-owned and family-operated *yakitori* (Japanese grilled chicken) joint that elevates simple grilled chicken skewers to unimaginable culinary heights. We love the wings, the neck, chicken skin, meatballs and the minced-chicken bowl topped with quail egg. It does livers, kidneys and hearts too. It's one of several tasty Asian joints in an area known as **Little Osaka** – a two block stretch of Sawtelle north of Olympic.

Pingtung
ASIAN $

22 [🍴] Map p56, G3

Our new favorite place to eat on Melrose is this pan-Asian market cafe where the dim sum (wild crab dumplings), seaweed and green papaya salads, and rice bowls piled with curried chicken and BBQ beef are all worthy of praise. They have an inviting back patio with ample seating, wi-fi and good beer on tap. ([📞]323-866-1866; www.pingtungla.com; 7455 Melrose Ave; dishes $6-12; [🕐]11:30am-10:30pm;)

Drinking

Bar Marmont
BAR

23 [🍷] Map p56, E1

Elegant, but not stuck up. Been around, yet still cherished. The famous, and wish-they-weres, still flock here for terrific martinis. If you time it right you might see Thom Yorke or perhaps Lindsay Lohan? Come midweek. Weekends are for amateurs. ([📞]323-650-0575; www.chateaumarmont.com/barmarmont.php; 8171 Sunset Blvd; [🕐]6pm-2am)

Comme Ca
BAR

24 [🍷] Map p56, D3

The brainy barmen serve prohibition-era cocktails – meaning they only use what was available during the 1920s and 1930s. No tropical fruits and, as one particularly surly barman says, 'no effing cranberry juice.' Penicillin blends scotch with ginger, honey and lemon strained over block ice, and the Mexican Firing Squad mixes tequila, muddled lime and grenadine. (www.commecarestaurant.com; 8479 Melrose Ave; ⏰5:30-11pm)

Abbey
CLUB

25 Map p56, C3

Once a humble coffee house, the Abbey has developed into WeHo's bar-club-restaurant of record. Always fun, it has so many different flavored martinis and mojitos that you'd think they were invented here, plus a full menu. Match your mood to the different spaces, from outdoor patio to goth lounge to chill room. (www.abbeyfoodandbar.com; 692 N Robertson Blvd; mains $9-13; ⏰11am-2am Mon-Thu, from 10am Fri, from 9am Sat & Sun)

Formosa Cafe
BAR

26 Map p56, H2

Humphrey Bogart and Clark Gable used to knock'em back at this dark rail-car watering hole. So authentically noir that scenes from *LA Confidential* were filmed here. Skip the Chinese food. (☎323-850-9050; 7156 Santa Monica Blvd; ⏰4pm-2am Mon-Fri, 6pm-2am Sat & Sun)

Entertainment

House of Blues
LIVE MUSIC

27 Map p56, E1

Frankly, there ain't much blues playing these days at this faux Mississippi Delta shack, but at least its small size and

Formosa Cafe

imaginative decor make it a neat place to catch bands of all stripes: headliners and up-and-comers, rock, reggae or hip-hop. (☎323-848-5100; www.hob.com; 8430 W Sunset Blvd)

Sundance Sunset Cinema
CINEMA

28 Map p56, F1

First there was a festival, then a channel, and now there is a burgeoning art-house cinema chain bearing the name of one of Redford's most famous characters. Enjoy a glass of wine and beer while you take in the latest unblockbuster. Screenings are all 21 and over. (☎323-654-2217; www.sundancecinemas.com; 8000 W Sunset Blvd; tickets $11-14)

BRENT WINEBRENNER/GETTY IMAGES ©

Understand
The Pink Palace

The **Beverly Hills Hotel** (www.beverlyhillshotel.com; 9641 Sunset Blvd) has served as unofficial hobnobbing headquarters of the industry elite since 1912. In the 1930s its Polo Lounge was a notorious hangout of Darryl F Zanuck, Spencer Tracy, Will Rogers and other lords of the polo crowd. Elizabeth Taylor bedded six of her eight husbands in various bungalows. Marilyn is reported to have 'bungalowed' both JFK and RFK here. After years of neglect, the Sultan of Brunei coughed up almost $300 million to reclaim her blush, lurid wink and ability to seduce the power players. For a time, scripts were once again read and deals cut in the Polo Lounge. Then Brunei adopted sharia law – despite the sultan's well-chronicled playboy exploits – and Hollywood outrage, given voice by noted feminist, Jay Leno, pinned it to the industry blacklist. Stay tuned.

Roxy
MUSIC VENUE

 29 Map p56, C2

A Sunset fixture since 1973, the Roxy has presented everyone from Miles Davis to David Bowie to Jane's Addiction, and still occasionally manages to book music that matters today. It's a small venue, so you'll be up close and personal with the bands. (☏310-276-2222; www.theroxyonsunset.com; 9009 W Sunset Blvd)

Groundlings
COMEDY

 30 Map p56 , H3

This improv school and company has launched Lisa Kudrow, Will Ferrell, Maya Rudolph and other top talent. Their sketch comedy and improv can be belly-achingly funny, especially on Thursdays when the main company, alumni and surprise guests get to riff together in *Cookin' with Gas*. (☏323-934-4747; www.groundlings.com; 7307 Melrose Ave; tickets $10-20)

Troubadour
LIVE MUSIC

 31 Map p56, B3

The celebrated 1957 rock hall launched a thousand careers, those of James Taylor and Tom Waits included, and was central to John Lennon's 'Lost Weekend in 1973.' It's still a great spot for catching tomorrow's headliners and appeals to beer-drinking music aficionados that keep attitude to a minimum. Come early to snag a seat on the balcony. No age limit. (www.troubadour.com; 9081 Santa Monica Blvd)

Comedy Store
COMEDY

32 Map p56, D1

There's no comedy club in the city with more street cred than Sammy and Mitzi Shore's Comedy Store on the strip. Sammy launched the club, but Mitzi was the one who brought in hot young comics such as Richard Pryor, George Carlin, Eddie Murphy, Robin Williams and David Letterman. These days [...] son, Pauly, runs it. (www.thecomedy[...] com; 8433 W Sunset Blvd)

Laugh Factory COMEDY

33 ⭐ Map p56, F1

The Marx Brothers used to keep offices at this long-standing club. It still gets some big names from time to time. (☎323-656-1336; www.laughfactory.com; 8001 W Sunset Blvd)

Shopping

Reformation FASHION

34 🔒 Map p56, E3

Here's classic, retro-inspired, fashionable outerwear that's eco-conscious without the granola. Their tag line is 'change the world without changing your style.' They get it done by using only pre-existing materials, which means no additional dying of fabrics and half the water use of other fashion brands. Everything is made locally downtown. (www.thereformation.com; 8253 Melrose Ave; ◷11am-7pm)

Rodeo Drive FASHION

35 🔒 Map p56, A5

It's pricey and pretentious, but no trip to LA would be complete without a saunter along Rodeo Dr, the famous three-block ribbon of style where sample-size fembots browse for **Escada** (www.escada.com; 250 N Rodeo Dr) and **Prada** (343 N Rodeo Dr). The latter's

flagship store at No 343 is a Rem Koolhaas–designed stunner lidded by a pitched-glass roof.

Book Soup BOOKS

36 🔒 Map p56, C2

A bibliophile's indie gem, sprawling and packed with entertainment, travel, feminist and queer studies, and eclectic and LA-based fiction, plus appearances by big-name authors. (☎310-659-3110; www.booksoup.com; 8818 W Sunset Blvd; ◷9am-10pm Mon-Sat, to 7pm Sun)

Fred Segal FASHION

37 🔒 Map p56, E3

Celebs and beautiful people circle for the very latest from Babakul, Aviator Nation and Robbi & Nikki at this warren of high-end boutiques under one impossibly chic but slightly snooty roof. The only time you'll see bargains (sort of) is during the two-week blowout sale in September. (☎323-651-4129; www.fredsegal.com; 8100 Melrose Ave; ◷10am-7pm Mon-Sat, noon-6pm Sun)

Wall Street Gallery ART

38 🔒 Map p56, C4

This new gallery is the domain of Mr Brainwash of *Exit Through the Gift Shop* fame. Whatever you may think of Banksy, Mr Brainwash or the film, it's worth stopping in to take a look for yourself. (☎424-279-9404; www. wall-streetgallery.com; 302 N Robertson Blvd; ◷noon-6pm & by appt)

Understand
Sole Music

Jeremy Sole, a working-class kid and former graffiti artist from Chicago, seems to be everywhere these days. He's producing original artists, editing old tracks and spinning at clubs and at his own monthly dance parties – theLift – which he hosts along with DJ Wiseacre. His base of operations is a funky Chinatown loft and his Wednesday night/Thursday morning midnight-to-3am shift on KCRW, an award-winning independent music oasis, is his springboard. Before electronic music had arrived, it was bumping on 89.9 FM (they also have a terrific smartphone app). But Sole doesn't cling to genre. His musical choice is wide reaching, fresh and funky and his voice intimate and inviting. Tune in, then find him somewhere out late spinning live. He's the guy with the bald head, yogi beard, bright smile and infectious grooves.

Chucks Vintage
VINTAGE

39 🔒 Map p56, F3

Easily the coolest – though not cheapest – vintage shop on Melrose. The hand-picked selection here is less about quantity and all about quality, from soft cotton tees and tasteful flannel to lace dresses and rugged denim and leather. The vintage signage on the walls is dope too. (☎323-653-5386; www.chucksvintage.com; 8012 Melrose Ave; ⏱noon-6pm Mon-Sat)

Diane von Furstenberg
FASHION

40 🔒 Map p56, D3

The LA flagship of the great and grand dame of fashion. Belgian born, von Furstenberg married into German royalty, divorced it, and became an American fashion icon thanks to – among other imagineerings – her signature wrap dress. If you be a fashion slave or spy, it's worth a wander.

(☎323-951-1947; www.dvf.com; 8407 Melrose Ave; ⏱11am-7pm Mon-Sat, noon-6pm Sun)

Joyrich
FASHION

41 🔒 Map p56, G3

A bright and funky boutique selling sportswear – blinged up and fashion-forward. There's Simpsons gear, leather shirts and jackets, reimagined football jerseys for girls, and cool handbags, clutches and backpacks. (www.joyrich.com; 7700 Melrose Ave; ⏱11am-8pm Mon-Sat, to 7pm Sun)

Slow
VINTAGE

42 🔒 Map p56, G3

Worth a stop for vintage shoppers. There's specs and hats, sun dresses from the '60s, some groovy tweeds and ragged old army threads. It specializes in one-of-a-kind pieces and leather goods. Prices are reasonable. (7474 Melrose Ave; ⏱noon-8pm Mon-Sat, to 7pm Sun)

Melrose Trading Post   FLEA MARKET

43 Map p56, F3

Here you'll find threads, jewelry, housewares and other offbeat items proffered by over 100 purveyors. It's held in the Fairfax High parking lot and proceeds help fund school programs. (http://melrosetradingpost.org; Fairfax High School, 7850 Melrose Ave; admission $2; ⊙9am-5pm Sun)

Pleasure Chest   EROTICA

44 Map p56, G2

LA's kingdom of kinkiness is filled with sexual hardware catering to every conceivable fantasy and fetish. Please, who doesn't need a penis beaker and a blow-up doll? Yeah, there's more naughty than nice. (☎323-650-1022; www.thepleasurechest.com; 7733 Santa Monica Blvd; ⊙10am-midnight Sun-Wed, to 1am Thu, to 2am Fri & Sat)

Nudie Jeans   DENIM

45 Map p56, F3

This is the only branded shop in North America from the Swedish-owned Nudie denim line. Jeans come in a variety of colors and range in price from $180 to $310, including free hemming and repair. The shop itself is a converted house outfitted with blackboard walls, one of which offers suggestions on when to wash your new denim. Short answer: every five to six months. Seriously. (www.nudiejeans.com; 710 N Edinburgh Ave; ⊙11am-7pm Mon-Sat, noon-6pm Sun)

CHRISTINA LEASE/GETTY IMAGES ©

Shopper on Rodeo Drive (p65)

Barneys New York   DEPARTMENT STORE

46 Map p56, A5

Four floors of straight-up chic. Prices are steep, so keep any eye out for one of its twice-annual warehouse sales for some cheap threads. There's a deli on the top floor that's worth trying, too. (☎310-276-4400; www.barneys.com; 9570 Wilshire Blvd; ⊙10am-7pm Mon-Wed, Fri & Sat, to 8pm Thu, noon-6pm Sun)

Top Sights
Getty Center

Getting There

🚗 **Car** The Getty Center is best accessed from the I-405, exit Getty Center Dr.

🚌 **Bus** You can also take the bus (Metro 761), which stops at the main gate.

In its billion-dollar, in-the-clouds perch, high above the city grit and grime, the Getty Center presents triple delights: a stellar art collection (Renaissance to David Hockney), Richard Meier's cutting-edge architecture (you'll love the jutting, cut-limestone bricks) and the visual splendor of seasonally changing gardens. On clear days, you can add breathtaking views of the city and ocean to the list.

Don't Miss

Central Garden

More than a few visitors spend more time outside the museum's hallowed halls than inside, thanks to the magnificent, Robert Irwin–designed central garden. The 134,000-sq-ft design includes a stream that winds through and past 500-plus plant varieties that twist into a labyrinthine swirl.

Permanent Collection

Although not everyone is captivated by the Getty's collection of European art, which spans the 17th to 20th centuries, there are some gems. Pieces from the baroque period can be found in the east pavilion, the west pavilion features neoclassical and Romantic sculpture and decorative arts, while the north pavilion is stuffed with medieval and Renaissance pieces. Must-sees include Van Gogh's *Irises,* Monet's *Wheatstacks,* Rembrandt's *The Abduction of Europa* and Titian's *Venus and Adonis.*

Rotating Exhibitions

Of course, if moldy old Euro art bores you, you'll almost certainly find something edgy and contemporary floating through on an exhibition basis. The center often hosts mind-bending installations and unique photography or multimedia exhibits.

☎ 310-440-7300

www.getty.edu

1200 Getty Center Dr, off I-405 Fwy

admission free

🕙 10am-5:30pm Tue-Fri & Sun, to 9pm Sat

☑ Top Tips

▶ A great time to visit is in the late afternoon after the crowds have thinned.

▶ Children can take a Family Tour, visit the interactive Family Room, borrow a kid-oriented audioguide or browse the special kid bookstore.

▶ Although most people drive (parking is $15), you can also take the bus (Metro 761), which stops at the main gate.

✕ Take a Break

The Getty Center is just 15 minutes from downtown Beverly Hills where you'll find LA's best Jewish deli, **Nate 'n Al** (p61) and, arguably, its best Mediterranean kitchen, **Momed** (p61).

Explore

Miracle Mile & Mid-City

The amorphous area we have called Mid-City encompasses the funky Fairfax District – once the domain of LA's Jews who moved here after WWII from Boyle Heights – Miracle Mile with Museum Row, and old-money Hancock Park with its grand mansions. This is where LA's history (or even pre-history) and its onrushing, creative, entrepreneurial future collide.

The Sights in a Day

☀ Enjoy a pastry and a coffee at **Republique** (p80) then hit **LACMA** (p74) to explore the permanent collections, rotating exhibitions and installations. If the kids get bored stroll them over to the gooey **La Brea Tar Pits & Page Museum** (p72) or step across the street to the **Petersen Automotive Museum** (pictured left; p78).

☀ Grown-ups should grab a New American lunch at **Ray's** (p81). Grown-ups with kids should head up to the **Grove** (p83) and the original **Farmers Market** (p81) for sustenance. Hipsters will appreciate the stylings of **American Rag Cie** (p85) on La Brea, and the stunning **Fahey/Klein Gallery** (p83). Skate punks and hip-hop freaks should make way to the Fairfax showrooms.

☾ At dinner, seafood lovers enjoy **Son of a Gun** (p79). Carnivores will want to descend on **Animal** (p79). Grab craft tequila at **El Carmen** (p81), then watch a show at **El Rey** (p82) or **Mint** (p83).

◉ Top Sights

La Brea Tar Pits & Page Museum (p72)

LACMA (p74)

♥ Best of Los Angeles

Eating
Ray's (p81)

Son of a Gun (p79)

Gallery Gazing
Wall Project (p78)

Drinking
El Carmen (p79)

Getting There

🚍 **Bus** MTA, LA's principal transit authority connects Mid-City with all other parts of town.

🚍 **Bus** Santa Monica's Big Blue Bus is also a useful network to the Westside and downtown.

Top Sights
La Brea Tar Pits & Page Museum

Even if you're not a fan of the *Ice Age* series, you'll likely have a ball at the unique Page Museum, an archaeological trove of skulls and bones unearthed at La Brea Tar Pits, one of the world's most famous fossil sites. Thousands of ice age critters met their maker between 40,000 and 10,000 years ago in crude oil bubbling from deep below Wilshire Blvd. A life-size mammoth family outside the museum dramatizes their fate.

👁 Map p76, E4

www.tarpits.org

5801 Wilshire Blvd

adult/child/student & senior $7/2/4.50

🕑 9:30am-5pm

American mastodon display at the Page Museum

Don't Miss

Project 23

During the construction of LACMA's new underground parking complex, 16 new fossil deposits were discovered, including a nearly complete skeleton of an adult mammoth. Paleontologists at the Page Museum helped preserve the fossilized bones, creating 23 fossil blocks. In 2008 excavation began and the fossils are now on public view, while excavators work seven days a week with hand tools such as dental picks, chisels, hammers and brushes to preserve and clean their bounty. This project will keep the lab busy for years.

Pit 91

Located just west of the Page Museum is the Pit 91 excavation site; before Project 23, this was the only active excavation site at Rancho La Brea during the past 40 years. Discovered during the 1913–15 excavations it was decided that this large cluster of fossils would be left in the tar as a 'showpiece.' Unfortunately, the site suffered repeated cave-ins and floods, and it was ultimately abandoned, with thousands of fossils still awaiting excavation. In the summer of 2014, paleontologists began digging back in!

Page Museum Collections

While all the giddy paleontologists and curious visitors converge around Pit 91 and Project 23, don't forget that within the Page Museum itself are 3.5 million fossil specimens of over 10,000 individuals representing 600-plus species of prehistoric mammals (90% of which were carnivores), birds (one of the largest collections of its kind in the world), flora, invertebrates, fish, amphibians and reptiles.

☑ Top Tips

▶ Although the museum does cost money, you can stroll through the park and admire the outdoor tar pits for free. Parking is $7.

▶ The Rancho La Brea tar pit is well known for preserving the largest and most-diverse collection of ice age plant and animal species ever discovered.

▶ Take your visit a step further and join one of the Page Museum's Family Overnight Trips, where the whole family can take part in fun educational games and activities and spend a night with the sabre-toothed tigers and woolly mammoths of the mind.

✖ Take a Break

Top off a visit to the tar pits with a meal at another family-friendly stopover, the original **Farmers Market** (p81). There's something here to satisfy even the fussiest mini-eaters among us.

Top Sights
Los Angeles County Museum of Art (LACMA)

A Renzo Piano–designed transformation made the 20-acre Los Angeles County Museum of Art (LACMA) campus, already the city's top art museum, even sexier. Here's an Aladdin's cave of paintings, sculpture and decorative arts stretching across ages and borders. Galleries are stuffed with all the major players – Rembrandt, Cézanne, Magritte, Mary Cassatt, Ansel Adams and David Hockney, to name a few – plus several millennia worth of global treasures.

👁 Map p76, E4

📞 323-857-6000

www.lacma.org

5905 Wilshire Blvd

adult/child $15/free

🕐 11am-5pm Mon, Tue & Thu, to 9pm Fri, 10am-7pm Sat & Sun

Urban Light by Chris Burden outside LACMA

Don't Miss

Japanese Art Pavilion
Pieces in this oh-so-Zen pavilion range in origin from 3000 BC to the 21st century. Here are Buddhist and Shinto sculpture, ancient ceramics and lacquerware, textiles and armor, and the epic Kasamatsu Shiro woodblock print, *Cherry Blossoms at Toshogu Shrine.*

Modern Art Collection
LACMA's permanent modern art collection is no slouch. Masterworks from luminaries like Picasso, Pissaro, Miró, Matisse, Magritte and Kandinsky are all here; some of them are from the notable Janice and Henri Lazarof Collection.

Rotating Exhibitions
In addition to its stellar permanent collections, LACMA rotates some fabulous special exhibitions. Recently it hosted a tremendous James Turrell exhibit featuring mind-bending fields of light that played on the brain and had Tinseltown buzzing.

☑ Top Tips

▶ Short on cash? Visit on the second Tuesday of the month and you can have access to all collections and exhibits for free.

▶ Friday nights are all about jazz. Throughout the year, world-class jazz musicians hold court in the plaza starting at 6pm. The sound and vibe are magnificent.

▶ LACMA also hosts film premieres, retrospectives, and public 'conversations' with heavyweight authors, filmmakers and thinkers.

✗ Take a Break

Once you pay the relatively steep admission, odds are you won't want to stray too far from campus when your stomach grumbles. Just step over to **Ray's** (p81) for New American cuisine, or find a cheap and cheerful food truck across the street.

| A | B | C | D |

For reviews see

◉ Top Sights   p72
◉ Sights   p78
✕ Eating   p79
🍷 Drinking   p81
★ Entertainment p82
🔒 Shopping   p83

1

Melrose Pl

Melrose Ave

Clinton St

N Sweetzer Ave

N Laurel Ave
N Edinburgh Ave
N Hayworth Ave
N Fairfax Ave

Rosewood Ave

S La Jolla Ave

N Crescent Heights Blvd

37🔒
8✕

BEVERLY CENTER DISTRICT

Oakwood Ave

N La Cienega Blvd

16✕

🍷 20

2

Beverly Blvd

Beverly Blvd

22🍷

S Edinburgh Ave
S Hayworth Ave

Farm Marke

34🔒

W 1st St

12✕

32✕ 31🔒
21🔒 36🔒

Gilm La

Burton Way

7✕ 11✕15✕29🔒 **W 3rd St**

19🍷

S Orlando Ave

14✕

3

Colgate Ave

Clifton Way

Colgate Ave

S Sweetzer Ave

S La Jolla Ave

S Crescent Heights Blvd

S Fairfax Ave

Wilshire Blvd

MID-CITY

4

Hanc Par

Wilshire Blvd

Petersen Automotive Museum ◉1

A-Muse

S Corning St

S La Cienega Blvd

La Cienega Park

S San Vicente Blvd

S Orange Grove Ave
S Ogden Dr

5

W Olympic Blvd

24★

W Olympic Blvd

Melrose Ave

**MELROSE/
LA BREA** Clinton St

N Genesee Ave
N Spaulding Ave
N Stanley Ave
N Curson Ave
N Sierra Bonita Ave
N Gardner St
N Vista St
N Martel Ave
N Fuller Ave
N Poinsettia Pl
N Alta Vista Blvd
N Formosa Ave
N Detroit St

N La Brea Ave

N Sycamore Ave

N Highland Ave

N Las Palmas Ave

**FAIRFAX
DISTRICT**

Oakwood Ave

6 ⊗

Beverly Blvd

🅿
2 **CBS
Television
City**

30 🔒

33 🔒

MID-CITY

25 ⭐

28 🔒

🅿 **27**

The Grove Dr

Pan
Pacific
Park

26 ⭐

S Gardner St
S Vista St
S Martel Ave
S Fuller Ave
S Poinsettia Pl
S Alta Vista Blvd

W 1st St

S Formosa Ave

35 🔒

S Orange Dr
S Mansfield Ave
S Citrus Ave
N Highland Ave
N Mc Cadden Pl
S Las Palmas Ave

W 2nd St

W 3rd St

S Alta Vista Blvd

S La Brea Ave

S Sycamore Ave

W 4th St

S McCadden Pl

**Los Angeles County
Museum of Art
(LACMA)** W 6th St

W 6th St

**La Brea Tar Pits
& Page Museum**

13 ⊗

4 **Wall
Project**

**Craft &
Folk Art
3 Museum**

23 ⭐

Wilshire Blvd

10 9 ⊗⊗

S Ridgeley Dr
S Dunsmuir Ave
S Cochran Ave
S Cloverdale Ave
S Detroit St

S Orange Dr
S Mansfield Ave
S Citrus Ave

S Alandele Ave
S Stanley Ave
S Curson Ave

Sights

Petersen Automotive Museum
MUSEUM

1 Map p76, D5

An ode to the auto, the Petersen Automotive Museum is a treat even to those who can't tell a piston from a carburetor. Start by ambling along a fun streetscape that reveals LA as the birthplace of gas stations, billboards, strip malls, drive-in restaurants and drive-in movie theaters. Then head upstairs to the hot rods, movie cars and celebrity-owned rarities. (www.petersen. org; 6060 Wilshire Blvd; adult/senior & student/ child $15/10/5; ⏱10am-6pm Tue-Sun; P)

CBS Television City
TV STUDIO

2 Map p76, E2

North of the Farmers Market is CBS, where game shows, talk shows, soap operas and other programs are taped, often before a live audience. (www.cbs. com; 7800 Beverly Blvd)

Craft & Folk Art Museum
MUSEUM

3 Map p76, E5

Zulu ceramics, Japanese *katagami* paper art, Palestinian embroidery – cultural creativity takes infinite forms at this well-respected museum where exhibits change every few months. Also check for upcoming kid-oriented workshops and storytelling sessions, usually on Saturdays. The gift store is one of the best in town. (www.cafam.org; 5814 Wilshire Blvd; adult/student & senior/child under 12 yr $7/5/free, 1st Wed of month free; ⏱11am-5pm Tue-Fri, noon-6pm Sat & Sun; ♿)

Wall Project
MUSEUM

4 Map p76, E5

Slabs of the old Berlin Wall – augmented by known street artists – are on display on the lawn of a Wilshire highrise across the street from LACMA as part of the global Wall Project, curated by the fabulous Wende Museum (www. wendemuseum.org) in Culver City. (www. wallproject.org; 5900 Wilshire Blvd; admission free)

A+D Museum
MUSEUM

5 Map p76, D5

A small Getty-sponsored space that keeps its finger on the pulse of emerging trends, people and products in the design and architecture community

---

Understand
Hancock Park

There's nothing quite like the old-money mansions flanking the tree-lined streets of Hancock Park, a genteel neighborhood roughly bounded by Highland, Rossmore, Melrose and Wilshire. LA's founding families, including the Dohenys and Chandlers, hired famous architects to build their pads in the 1920s, and to this day some celebrities, including Kiefer Sutherland, make their homes here.

from its base near the Petersen Automotive Museum. (www.aplusd.org; 6032 Wilshire Blvd; adult/senior & student $5/2.50; ⊙11am-5pm Tue-Fri, noon-6pm Sat & Sun)

Eating

Ita Cho   JAPANESE $$

6 Map p76, F2

Simply put, some of the best Japanese available in Los Angeles. Order any of their small plates, but don't miss the *nasu miso* (eggplant coated in sweet miso sauce), the buttery *enoki*, the broiled *unagi* (eel) and anything sashimi. Celeb sightings happen here. (☎323-938-9009; www.itachorestaurant.com; 7311 Beverly Blvd; dishes $6-20; ⊙11:30am-2:30pm & 5:30-10:30pm Mon-Fri, from 6pm Sat, 5-10pm Sun; P)

Son of a Gun   SEAFOOD $$$

7 Map p76, B3

If you love seafood, head straight for this creative kitchen where they glaze and grill kampachi collars, sear octopus with chiles, make a mean lobster roll, a terrific linguine and clams, and plate their burrata with *uni* (sea urchin). (☎323-782-9033; www.sonofagunrestaurant.com; 8370 W 3rd St; dishes $8-27; ⊙11:30am-2:30pm Mon-Fri, 6-11pm Sun-Thu, to midnight Fri & Sat)

Animal   MEAT $$$

8 Map p76, D2

Begin with chicken-liver toast or spicy beef tendons (which may be dipped in a *pho* sauce), then get the gnocchi drenched in six-hour, slow-cooked bolognese, or crispy pig's head, veal tongue or rabbit legs. We know it sounds intimidating, but carnivorous foodies pray at the Animal altar. (☎323-782-9225; www.animalrestaurant.com; 435 N Fairfax Ave; dishes $3-68; ⊙6-11pm Sun-Thu, to midnight Fri & Sat)

Milk Jar Cookies   COOKIES $

9 Map p76, F5

Once you get over the deliciously stunning scent of freshly baked cookies (it takes a moment) you can get around to the business of choosing a chocolate chip, rocky road, banana split, chocolate pecan caramel or white chocolate raspberry cookie. Pair it with milk, coffee or salted caramel ice cream. (www.milkjarcookies.com; 5466 Wilshire Blvd; cookies $3; ⊙11am-8pm Tue-Thu, to 11pm Fri & Sat, noon-5pm Sun)

Yuko Kitchen   JAPANESE $$

10 Map p76, F5

This adorable Japanese cafe just off Wilshire Blvd serves sashimi salads, udon and rice bowls piled with taco-seasoned ground beef, grilled tofu, spicy salmon and smelt eggs, or albacore sashimi. They also make terrific desserts. Staff are lovely; there is seating inside and out. (☎323-933-4020; www.yukokitchen.com; 5484 Wilshire Blvd; mains $10-15; ⊙11am-9:30pm Mon-Sat)

Food stand inside the Original Farmers Market

Joan's on Third

CAFE **$$**

11 🍴 Map p76, C3

One of the first market cafes in the LA area is still one of the best. The coffee and pastries are divine and the deli churns out tasty gourmet sandwiches and salads. Hence all the happy people eating alfresco on buzzy Third St. (☎323-655-2285; www.joansonthird.com; 8350 W 3rd St; mains $10-16; ⏱8am-8pm Mon-Sat, to 7pm Sun; 🍴🖫)

AOC

ITALIAN **$$$**

12 🍴 Map p76, A3

It's moved slightly west, but the small plates and terrific wines (over 50 of which can be ordered by the glass) are all here. Expect artisanal cheeses, homemade terrines and roast clams with green garlic. They even roast whole chickens ($42) and racks of lamb ($70), which serve two or more. (☎323-653-6359; www.aocwinebar.com; 8700 W 3rd St; small plates $9-17, mains $28-40; ⏱11:30am-11pm Mon-Fri, from 10am Sat, 10am-10pm Sun)

Republique

CONTINENTAL **$$$**

13 🍴 Map p76, G4

A design gem with the gourmet ambition to match. The old Campaline interior is still an atrium restaurant with stone arches, a brightly lit front end scattered with butcher-block tables, and a marble bar peering into an open kitchen. The menu changes daily but may include a pumpkin agnolotti, crab risotto, pig's head and lentils, and braised short rib. (☎310-362-6115; www.republiquela.com; 624 S La Brea; mains $18-32; ⏱8am-4pm Mon-Sat, 6-10pm Mon-Wed, to 11pm Thu-Sat)

Mercado

MEXICAN **$$**

14 🍴 Map p76, D3

Terrific *nuovo*-Mexican food served in white-washed brick environs, with dangling birdcage chandeliers and a terrific marble tequila bar. The slow-cooked *carnitas* (braised pork) melt in your mouth. They also spit-roast beef, grill sweet corn, and fold tasty tacos and enchiladas. Their *hora feliz* (happy hour) is among the best in the city. (☎323-944-0947; www.mercadorestaurant.com; 7910 W 3rd St; ⏱5-10pm Mon-Wed, to 11pm Thu & Fri, 4-11pm Sat, 10am-3pm & 4-10pm Sun)

Mama's Secret

TURKISH $

15 Map p76, C3

A delightful Turkish cafe where tables spill from a cheery interior onto the sidewalk. The gyro is wrapped in freshly baked lavash, the burger is made with a Mediterranean meatball patty and *gozleme* (flat breads) are filled with spinach and feta or spicy *soujouk* (sausage) and ground beef. They do all the typical *mezes* (hummus, tabouleh etc), too. (323-424-3482; www.mamassecretbakery.com; 8314 W 3rd St; mezes $5-8, mains $10-14; 8am-8pm Mon-Sat, to 6pm Sun)

Plan Check

PUB $$

16 Map p76, D2

Modern American comfort food is their jam: think portobello mushrooms stuffed with crispy kale, salmon pastrami, short-rib pot roast and damn good fried chicken. The burgers rock, too. Check the blackboards for specials before you order. That's also where you'll find the current beer list. Eight of their taps are taken over by a single buzz-worthy microbrew each month. (323-288-6500; www.plancheck.com; 351 N Fairfax Ave; mains $9-15; 11:30am-11pm Sun-Thu, to 1am Fri & Sat)

Ray's

NEW AMERICAN $$$

17 Map p76, E4

They change the menu twice daily, but if they offer it, order the shrimp and grits. It's rich and buttery floating with chunks of andouille sausage, okra and two king prawns. Their burrata melts with tang, the yellowtail collar is crisp and moist, and the bacon-wrapped rabbit sausage will wow you. (323-857-6180; www.raysandstarkbar.com; 5905 Wilshire Blvd; dishes $11-27; 11:30am-3pm & 5-10pm Mon-Fri, from 10am Sat & Sun; P; MTA 20)

Original Farmers Market

MARKET $

18 Map p76, D3

The Farmers Market is a great spot for a casual meal any time of day, especially if the rug rats are tagging along. There are lots of options here, from gumbo to Singapore-style noodles to tacos. (www.farmersmarketla.com; 6333 W 3rd St; mains $6-12; 9am-9pm Mon-Fri, to 8pm Sat, 10am-7pm Sun; P)

Drinking

El Carmen

BAR

19 Map p76, C3

A pair of mounted bull heads and *lucha libre* (Mexican wrestling) masks create an over-the-top 'Tijuana North' look and pull in an industry-heavy crowd at LA's ultimate tequila and mescal tavern (over 100 to choose from). (8138 W 3rd St; 5pm-2am Mon-Fri, from 7pm Sat & Sun)

Roger Room

BAR

20 Map p76, B2

Cramped but cool. Too cool even to have a sign out front. When hand-crafted, throwback cocktails first migrated west and south from New York and San Fran, they landed here. (www.therogerroom.com; 370 N La Cienega Blvd; ⏱6pm-2am Mon-Fri, 7pm-2am Sat, 8pm-2am Sun)

Churchill   PUB

21 🚇 Map p76, B3

Set on the ground floor of the Orlando hotel, this fun pub has an inviting outdoor patio, seating upstairs and down, and they pour craft suds and cocktails. The food is a slight step above pub grub, and you can catch a fun crowd day or night. (☎323-655-8384; www.the-churchill.com; 8384 W 3rd St; ⏱7am-midnight Sun-Thu, to 2am Fri & Sat; 🛜)

Beverly Hills Juice Club   JUICE BAR

22 🚇 Map p76, B2

This hippie classic, and the first on the LA health-food, raw-power bandwagon, started out on Sunset when Tom Waits

and Rickie Lee Jones used to stumble in between shows. It still attracts an in-the-know crowd craving wheatgrass shots and banana-manna shakes. Get yours with a shot of algae. No, seriously. (www.beverlyhillsjuice.com; 8382 Beverly Blvd; ⏱7am-6pm Mon-Fri, 9am-6pm Sat)

Entertainment

Largo at the
Coronet   LIVE MUSIC, PERFORMING ARTS

Largo, ever since its early days on Fairfax Ave, has been progenitor of high-minded pop culture (it nurtured Zach Galifianakis to stardom). Now part of the Coronet Theatre complex, they bring edgy comedy (Sarah Silverman, Jon Hodgman), and nourishing night music (Brad Meldau and his jazz piano to Andrew Bird's acoustic ballads). It's near the Roger Room (see 20 🚇 Map p76, B2; ☎310-855-0530; www.largo-la.com; 366 N La Cienega Blvd)

El Rey   MUSIC VENUE

23 ⭐ Map p76, F5

An old art deco dancehall decked out in red velvet and chandeliers and flaunting an awesome sound system and excellent sightlines. Although it can hold 800 people, it feels quite small. Performance-wise, it's popular with indie acts like Black Joe Lewis and the Honeybears, and the rockers who love them. (www.theelrey.com; 5515 Wilshire Blvd; cover varies)

Local Life
Larchmont Ave

Who dropped Mayberry in the middle of Los Angeles? With its stroller-friendly coffee shops, locally owned boutiques and low-key patios, Larchmont is an oasis of square normality bordering a desert of Hollywood hipness. Gourmet sandwiches from **Larchmont Village Wine, Spirits & Cheese Shop** (☎323-856-8699; www.larchmontvillagewine.com; 223 N Larchmont Blvd; ⏱10am-7pm Mon-Wed, to 8pm Thu-Sat) are perfect for a Hollywood Bowl picnic.

Mint   MUSIC VENUE

24 ⭐ Map p76, B5

Built in 1937, Mint is an intimate, historic venue. Legends such as Ray Charles and Stevie Wonder played here on the come up and axeman Ben Harper got his start here too. Expect a packed slate of terrific jazz, blues and rock shows, sensational sound, and you'll never be more than 30ft from the performance stage. (www.themintla.com; 6010 W Pico Blvd; cover $5-25)

Acme Comedy Theatre   COMEDY

25 ⭐ Map p76, G2

Not the most famous sketch-comedy theater, but big names like Adam Corolla, Joel McHale and Russell Brand have appeared on stage. (www.acmecomedy.com; 135 N La Brea Ave; tickets $15-30; ⏲Thu-Sat)

Pacific Theatres at the Grove   CINEMA

26 ⭐ Map p76, E3

This is a fancy all-stadium, 14-screen multiplex with comfy reclining seats, wall-to-wall screens and superb sound. The Monday Morning Mommy Movies series (11am) gives the diaper-bag brigade a chance to catch a flick with their tot but without hostile stares from non-breeders. (www.pacifictheatres.com; 189 The Grove Dr; adult/senior/child $13/9/9.50; 🚻)

ALBERTO E RODRIGUEZ/GETTY IMAGES ©

Largo at the Coronet

Shopping

Grove   OUTDOOR MALL

27 🔒 Map p76, E3

This faux-Italian palazzo is one of LA's most popular shopping destinations with 40 brand-name stores, a fountain and a trolley rolling down the middle. (☎888-315-8883; www.thegrovela.com; 189 The Grove Dr; ⏲10am-9pm Mon-Thu, to 10pm Fri & Sat, 11am-8pm Sun; MTA 16)

Fahey/Klein Gallery   GALLERY

28 🔒 Map p76, G2

The best in vintage and contemporary fine-art photography by icons such as

Annie Leibovitz, Bruce Weber and the late, great rock 'n' roll shutterbug, Jim Marshall. It even has his lesser-known civil rights catalog in its vast archives. (www.faheykleingallery.com; 148 S La Brea Ave; ⏱10am-6pm Tue-Sat)

DL Rhein
ANTIQUES

29 Map p76, C3

A cluttered den of interior delights from antique glass to furniture, including special limited-edition pieces. There's silver and crystal, scented candles and baking trays stuffed with jewelry. The entire shop is a terrific browse. (☎323-653-5590; www.dlrhein.com; 8300½ W 3rd St; ⏱10am-6pm Mon-Fri, 11am-6pm Sat, to 5pm Sun)

Espionage
VINTAGE, INTERIORS

30 Map p76, F2

A fabulous boutique blessed with a tasteful melange of new and vintage goods. Its jewelry is fantastic, as are the chunky vintage perfume bottles and ashtrays. The leather chairs work perfectly with the brass-and-glass end tables, and it offers a collection of vintage couture clothing sold on consignment. (☎323-272-4942; www.espionagela.com; 7456 Beverly Blvd; ⏱11am-6pm Mon, to 7pm Tue-Fri, 10:30am-7pm Sat, to 6pm Sun)

Lotta Boutique
FASHION

31 Map p76, B3

Boho-chic style is served at this single-label shop where you'll find handmade Lotta Stensson gowns and baby doll dresses, unique jewelry and hats popular among such glitterati as Beyoncé. (www.lottanyc.com; 8372 W 3rd St; ⏱11am-7pm Mon-Sat, noon-5pm Sun)

Le Labo
PERFUMERY

32 Map p76, B3

The West Hollywood branch of this noted fragrance lab based in New York offers 14 fragrances, including one you may only purchase here. All are alchemized with natural oils such as patchouli, vetiver, iris and ylang-ylang. Simply pick the one you like and they'll make a bottle fresh for you. They have addictive shower gel, body lotion, massage oil and balm, too. (☎323-782-0411; www.lelabofragrances.com; 8385 W 3rd St; ⏱11am-7pm Mon-Sat, to 5pm Sun)

Gibson

VINTAGE INTERIORS

33 🔒 Map p76, F2

If you love vintage interiors, step into this gem of a gallery, where (almost) everything from vintage baseball bats to armchairs and desks to the art on the walls was birthed in another era (or reproduced to look that way). It's owned and operated by noted designer Gary Gibson, who operates his interior-design studio out back. (📞323-934-4248; www.garygibson.com; 7350 Beverly Blvd; ⏱9am-6pm Mon-Fri, 11am-5pm Sat)

Polkadots & Moonbeams

BOOKS

34 🔒 Map p76, A2

Like a burst of sunlight on a cloudy day, enjoy this whimsical yet exceptional vintage women's wear shop, stocked with affordable designer dresses, shades, scarves and hats. There's another branch with some new labels a few doors down, but the vintage shop is where it's at. (📞323-655-3880; www.polkadotsandmoonbeams.com; 8367 W 3rd St; ⏱11am-7pm Mon-Sat, noon-6pm Sun)

American Rag Cie

VINTAGE

35 🔒 Map p76, G3

This industrial-flavored warehouse-sized space has kept trend-hungry stylistas looking fabulous since 1985. Join them in their hunt for secondhand leather, denim, T-shirts and shoes. It also has some new gear. It's not cheap, but it is one hell of a browse. We particularly enjoyed the period homewares in the Maison Midi wing. (📞323-935-

3154; www.amrag.com; 150 S La Brea; ⏱10am-9pm Mon-Sat, noon-7pm Sun)

OK

GALLERY

36 🔒 Map p76, C3

A concrete-floor emporium of quirky cool, OK has art and cookbooks, bar kits and paper lanterns, glass radiometers (measures light), pens and notebooks. But you might enjoy the jewelry and glassware most of all. (www.okthestore.com; 8303 W 3rd St; ⏱11am-6:30pm Mon-Sat, noon-6pm Sun)

Supreme

FASHION

37 🔒 Map p76, D2

When we rolled by, this beloved skate/punk/hip-hop mash-up of a label had just reopened their doors with fans lined up for half a block to get a taste of the new line. So yes, it's a thing. Also, they have a half-pipe in the store, and that's maybe the best of things. (📞323-655-6205; supremenewyork.com; 439 N Fairfax Ave)

Kayo

FASHION

38 🔒 Map p76, D1

This hip-hop skater retailer on Fairfax is set in a converted bank building and they have the vault to prove it. They deal in labels such as Organika and have some of the best and most interesting T-shirt designs on the block. They also hock decks, trucks and wheels if you want a ride. (www.thekayostore.com; 464 N Fairfax Ave; ⏱11am-7pm Mon-Sat, from noon Sun)

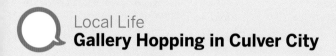

Local Life
Gallery Hopping in Culver City

Getting There

🚗 Culver City is accessible via Robertson Blvd from Mid-City and from Washington Blvd in Venice.

🚌 The Culver City bus line serves areas in the city, Santa Monica, Venice and West LA.

A decade ago Culver City bloomed from its bland, semi-suburban studio-town roots into a stylish yet unpretentious destination for fans of art, culture and food, and it happened organically. Then the 2008 recession hit and Culver City buckled. But the roots of groovy stayed alive, and this 'hood has come back stronger than ever.

1 Gallery Gazing

A major US art player and juggernaut of the Culver City arts district, **Blum & Poe** (www.blumandpoe.com; 2727 S La Cienega Blvd; ⏲10am-6pm Tue-Sat) reps international stars Takashi Murakami, Sam Durant and Sharon Lockhart.

2 Roaming the District

The Helms complex marks the beginning of Culver City's vital **Arts District** (www.ccgalleryguide.com; La Cienega Blvd), which runs east along Washington to La Cienega and up one block to Venice Blvd.

3 Something Strange

Arguably LA's most intriguing exhibition space, the **Museum of Jurassic Technology** (📞310-836-6131; www.mjt.org; 9341 Venice Blvd; suggested donation adult/student & senior/under 12 yr $5/3/free; ⏲2-8pm Thu, noon-6pm Fri-Sun) has nothing to do with dinosaurs and even less with technology. Instead, you'll find madness nibbling at your synapses as you try to read meaning into mind-bending displays about Cameroonian stink ants and microscopic pope sculpture.

4 Eames on LSD

Like Eames on acid, the **Greg Fleishman Studio** (www.greggfleishman.com; 3850 Main St; ⏲11am-7pm Wed-Sat) puts the 'fun' in functional with his ingenious solid birch plywood furniture bent, carved and spiraled into springy forms. Lumbar support never looked or felt so...mind opening.

5 Taste of the Town

There's no shortage of creative kitchens in Culver. **Akasha** (📞310-845-1700; www.akasharestaurant.com; 9543 Culver Blvd; mains $8-22; ⏲11:30am-2:30pm & 5:30-9:30pm Mon-Thu, to 10:30pm Fri & Sat, 10:30am-2:30pm & 5-9pm Sun; 🚻) takes all-natural ingredients and turns them into tasty small plates, such as bacon-wrapped dates stuffed with chorizo, and big ones like the zinfandel-braised short rib. **Lukshon** (📞310-202-6808; www.lukshon.com; 3239 Helms Ave; dishes $9-31; ⏲noon-3pm & 5:30-10pm Tue-Thu, to 10:30 Fri & Sat) serves upscale Southeast Asian flavors in high design environs, and you can get craft beer and sourdough crusted pizza at the slab marble bar at **Wild Craft** (📞310-815-8100; www.wildcraftpizza.com; 9725 Culver Blvd; mains $11-16; ⏲noon-9pm Sun & Mon, to 10pm Tue-Thu, to 11pm Fri & Sat).

6 Kirk Douglas Theatre

An old-timey movie house has been recast as the 300-seat **Kirk Douglas Theatre** (www.centertheatergroup.org; 9820 Washington Blvd). Since opening in 2004, it has become an integral part of Culver City's growing arts scene, showcasing new plays by local playwrights.

Explore

Santa Monica

Here's where real-life Lebowskis sip White Russians alongside martini-swilling Hollywood producers. Where surf rats, skate punks, soccer moms, yoga freaks and street performers congregate along a sublime coastline, lapping at the heels of a chaparral-draped mountain range. Welcome to Santa Monica – LA's cute, alluring, hippie-chic little sister, its karmic counterbalance and, to some, its salvation.

The Sights in a Day

☀ Enjoy breakfast at the beloved **Huckleberry** (p96), where the bakery is always rocking and the coffee is sublime. Then walk down Wilshire to the bluffs at **Palisades Park** (p94) and take it all in. Continue staring out to sea as you stroll south to the **Santa Monica Pier** (p90). If you have kids, hop the Ferris wheel at **Pacific Park** (p91). Otherwise walk to the end of the pier with the anglers, then down to the sand on **Santa Monica Beach**, where you can stick your toes in cool Pacific blue or rent a bicycle or Rollerblades from **Perry's** (p91).

☼ Hit **Tacos Por Favor** (p96) for authentic *taqueria* flavor then stroll and shop the **Third Street Promenade** (p101). As the afternoon grows late, make your way to Main St and the **California Heritage Museum** (p94) then back to the beach for sunset.

☾ When dinner beckons, make your way to **Bar Pintxo** (p95), where the tapas and wine are transcendent. If it's Wednesday, head to **Harvelle's** (p99) for the House of Vibe All-Stars. Otherwise, pile into the **Basement Tavern** (p98) on Main St.

 Top Sights

💙 **Best of Los Angeles**

Getting There

🚌 **Bus** MTA, LA's principal transit authority, connects Santa Monica with all other parts of town.

🚌 **Bus** Big Blue Bus is the best choice for transport within Santa Monica, south to Venice and east to Westwood, and downtown.

Top Sights
Santa Monica Pier & Beach

Dating back to 1908, the Santa Monica Pier is the city's most compelling landmark. There are carnival games, a vintage carousel, a Ferris wheel, a roller coaster and an aquarium, but the thing here is the view. Walk to the edge, lose yourself in the rolling blue-green sea or make your way to the golden sand that extends in a gentle arc for miles.

⊙ Map p92, A4

☎ 310-458-8900

www.santamonicapier.org

Don't Miss

Pacific Park

A small amusement park popular with kids, **Pacific Park** (☎310-260-8744; www.pacpark.com; ⊙11am-9pm Sun-Thu, to midnight Fri & Sat Jun-Aug, shorter hours Sep-May; 👪) has a solar-powered Ferris wheel, kiddie rides, midway games, a trapeze school and food concessions. Check the website for discount coupons.

Original Muscle Beach

South of the pier is the **Original Muscle Beach**, where the Southern California exercise craze began in the mid-20th century, and new equipment now draws a new generation of fitness fanatics.

Beach Sports

Grab a bike, board, and a pair of blades or hit a beach-volleyball court and enjoy the beach like most Californians do, by getting active. **Perry's Café** (☎310-939-0000; www.perryscafe.com; Ocean Front Walk; mountain bikes & Rollerblades per hr/day $10/30, bodyboards per hr/day $7/17; ⊙9:30am-5:30pm) is the place to seek rentals. Its locations provide immediate access to the South Bay Bicycle Trail.

☑ Top Tips

▶ The pier comes alive with the Twilight Dance Series, a free concert program on Thursday nights in summer. The lineup is generally eclectic and usually satisfying.

▶ A section of the South Bay Bicycle Trail runs along the beach – pick it up under the pier and ride all the way down to Redondo Beach if you're feeling strong.

▶ For cerebral pursuits, settle in at a first-come, first-served chess table at the International Chess Park, just south of the pier.

✕ Take a Break

Native Angelenos are familiar with the following summer pairing: **Bay Cities** (p96) sandwiches and the Santa Monica Beach. Here's what to do. Hit LA's best deli early (before the crowds become unmanageable) and tote your grub, beach blanket and beverages to the golden sand for a classic beach picnic.

Santa Monica Fwy

Woodlawn Cemetery

Woodlawn Cemetery

Santa Monica College

26

For reviews see

◉ Top Sights	p90
◉ Sights	p94
❽ Eating	p95
● Drinking	p98
❸ Entertainment	p99
❶ Shopping	p100

16th St

14th St

Euclid St

Pearl St

Pine St

Ocean Park Blvd

11th St

10th St

Bay St

Lincoln Blvd

Lincoln Blvd

Santa Monica High School

6th St

Hollister Ave

Hill St

Ashland Ave

4th St

3rd St

Marine St

Pico Blvd

Santa Monica Visitor Center

4th St

California Heritage Museum

Jadis

2nd St

Main St

ain St

23

cean Ave

Bay St

17

Neilson Way

20

19 ❶ 35
29

18 ❽ 4

5

28

Streetcraft LA

Barnard Way

Speedway

South Bay Bicycle Trail

Santa Monica Bay

5

6

7

8

A

B

C

D

E

Sights

Bergamot Station Arts Center
ARTS CENTER

1 ⊙ Map p92, E4

Art fans gravitate inland toward this avant-garde center, which houses 35 galleries and the progressive **Santa Monica Museum of Art** (www.smmoa. org; 2525 Michigan Ave; donation adult/senior & student $5/3; ⊙11am-6pm Tue-Sat) in a former trolley stop. (www.bergamot station.com; 2525 Michigan Ave; ⊙10am-6pm Tue-Fri, 11am-5:30pm Sat; Ⓟ)

Palisades Park
PARK

2 ⊙ Map p92, B2

Perhaps it's appropriate that Route 66, America's most romanticized byway, ends at this gorgeous cliffside park perched dramatically on the edge of the continent. Stretching 1.5 miles north from the pier, this palm-dotted greenway is tops with joggers and people-watchers. (cnr Colorado Blvd & Ocean Ave; admission free; ⊙5am-midnight)

California Heritage Museum
MUSEUM

3 ⊙ Map p92, B7

For a trip back in time, check out the latest exhibit at this museum housed in one of Santa Monica's few surviving grand Victorian mansions – this one was built in 1894. Curators do a fine job presenting pottery, colorful tiles, craftsman furniture, folk art, vintage surfboards and other fine collectibles

in as dynamic a fashion as possible. (www.californiaheritagemuseum.org; 2612 Main St; adult/student & senior/child under 12 yr $10/5/free; ⊙11am-4pm Wed-Sun; Ⓟ)

Jadis
MUSEUM

4 ⊙ Map p92, B7

Don't miss this homespun, steampunk paradise. It's a museum grinding with old gears and spare-part robots, antique clocks, concept planes and cars, old globes and lanterns – most of which were once film props. The prized piece is the robot from the famed 1927 film *Metropolis*. (2701 Main St; admission $1; ⊙noon-5pm Sun)

Streetcraft LA
GRAFFITI GALLERY

5 ⊙ Map p92, B8

A cooperative of street artists, it started as a nonprofit taking vandal artists and teaching them the skills to become working artists. It does occasional art openings, live graffiti demos and offers street art tours (per person $40) of Santa Monica and Venice. (www.streetcraftla.com; 2912 Main St)

Tongva Park
PARK

6 ⊙ Map p92, B4

A new green space that connects Ocean Ave to the Santa Monica Civic Center area. Well-lit and maintained, here are palms and agave groves, cascading fountains and amphitheater seating, trim lawns and an ergonomic playground for tots. (1615 Ocean Ave; ⊙6am-11pm)

Palisades Park

Eating

Bar Pintxo
SPANISH $$

 Map p92, B3

Here's a classic Barcelona-inspired tapas bar. It's small, it's cramped, it's a bit loud and a lot of fun. Tapas include pork belly braised in duck fat, lamb *albondigas* (meatballs), a tremendous seared calamari, and the paella is can't-miss – it's served as a tapas ($9) on Tuesdays. (☎310-458-2012; www. barpintxo.com; 109 Santa Monica Blvd; tapas $4-16, paella $30; ☸4-10pm Mon-Wed, to 11pm Thu, to midnight Fri, noon-midnight Sat, to 10pm Sun)

Milo & Olive
ITALIAN $$

 Map p92, E2

We love them for their small batch wines, incredible pizzas and terrific breakfasts (creamy polenta and poached eggs anyone?), breads and pastries, all of which you may enjoy at the marble bar or shoulder to shoulder with new friends at one of two common tables. It's a cozy neighborhood joint, so they don't take reservations. (☎310-453-6776; www. miloandolive.com; 2723 Wilshire Blvd; dishes $7-20; ☸7am-11pm)

Rustic Canyon
CALIFORNIAN $$$

9 Map p92, D3

Almost all the ingredients come from local organic producers, which means the menu shifts with availability, but count on two handmade pasta dishes and an assortment of stunning small plates. The burger is divine. (☎310-393-7050; www.rusticcanyonwinebar.com; 1119 Wilshire Blvd; dishes $12-33; ⏱5:30-10:30pm Sun-Thu, to 11pm Fri & Sat)

Huckleberry
CAFE $$

10 Map p92, C3

The second in a growing epicurean family from the couple behind Rustic Canyon, and arguably its most popular, here Zoe Nathan devises some of the most exquisite pastries available in the city. Think crostatas bursting with blueberries, maple bacon biscuits, and pumpkin-and-ginger tea cakes. (www.huckleberrycafe.com; 1014 Wilshire Blvd; mains $10-14; ⏱8am-8pm Mon-Fri, to 5pm Sat & Sun)

Blue Plate Oysterette
SEAFOOD $$

11 Map p92, B3

There's only one reason to ignore a raw bar that includes a ceviche of the day, delectable oysters, prawns and clams – you've ordered the lobster roll or the lobster mac 'n' cheese. (☎310-576-3474; www.blueplatesantamonica.com; 1355 Ocean Ave; dishes $9-22; ⏱11:30am-10pm Sun-Thu, to 11pm Fri & Sat)

Bay Cities
ITALIAN DELI $

12 Map p92, C4

Not just the best Italian deli in LA, this is arguably the best deli, period. With sloppy, spicy godmothers (piled with salami, mortadella, coppacola, ham, prosciutto, provolone, and pepper salad), house-roasted tri-tip, tangy salads, imported meats, cheeses, breads, oils and extras. Get your sandwich with the works. And, yes, it's worth the wait. (www.baycitiesitaliandeli.com; 1517 Lincoln Blvd; sandwiches $5-9; ⏱9am-7pm Tue-Sat, to 6pm Sun)

Sugarfish
SUSHI $$

13 Map p92, B3

The Santa Monica shingle of a popular sushi chain imagined by LA's reformed Sushi Nazi, Chef Nozawa. You can order à la carte or one of the three Trust Me menus which are reasonably priced, fulfilling and delicious. Their special rice recipe offers just a hint of sweetness, and don't miss out on the blue crab roll. Phenomenal. (sugarfishsushi.com; 1345 2nd St; meals from $20; ⏱11:30am-10pm Mon-Sat, noon-9pm Sun)

Tacos Por Favor
MEXICAN $

14 Map p92, D5

This is a no-nonsense taco joint, a dingy hole-in-the-wall, smoky, hot and crowded. It also happens to serve the best shrimp, chicken and carne asada tacos and burritos in town. Hence the lunchtime crush. (www.tacosporfavor.net; 1406 Olympic Blvd; dishes $4.50-11; ⏱8am-8pm)

Real Food Daily

VEGAN $$

15 Map p92, C4

Vegan-cooking guru Ann Gentry gives meat and dairy substitutes an interesting inflection. The lentil-walnut pâté is a complex starter and classics like the Salisbury seitan (a wheat gluten-based dish) and tempeh tacos feed the body and soul. (☎310-451-7544; www.realfood.com; 514 Santa Monica Blvd; mains $12-15; ☺lunch & dinner; ☒)

Mercado

MEXICAN $$

16 Map p92, B4

Our favorite happy hour cabana, this downtown Santa Monica location was their first, and it's only at happy hour when they do exquisite *carnitas* tacos that melt in your mouth. But they mix excellent margaritas and have a killer tequila list all the time. This is upscale Mexican: expect dishes such as *arracherra* skewers and scallops encrusted with pumpkin seeds. (☎310-526-7121; www.mercadorestaurant. com; 1416 4th St; small plates $9-17, large plates $17-25; ☺5-10pm Mon-Wed, to 11pm Thu & Fri, 4-11pm Sat, to 10pm Sun)

M Street Kitchen

CALIFORNIAN $$

A wildly popular breakfast and lunch choice, with abundant sunshine patio seating, that transforms farmers market produce and all-natural ingredients into comfortable creations like pulled chicken nachos, terrific fried-egg sandwiches at breakfast, housemade veggie burgers at lunch and soft taco platters that have their own devout cult following. Near Stella Barra (see 17 Map p92, B6) pizza joint. (☎310-396-9145; www.mstreetkitchen.com; 2000 Main St; mains $7-21; ☺8am-10pm Sun-Thu, to 11pm Fri & Sat; ☒)

Stella Barra

PIZZA $$

17 Map p92, B6

One of our favorite places on Main, they do a white pizza loaded with crispy kale, and another with prosciutto and egg on a bed of mozzarella and gruyere. They make their own pork sausage and the salads are tasty. Even the breakfast pizzas work. So do the $5 bloodies. The sleek but well-lit interior, rectangular island bar and fun-loving staff lure a great weekend and after-work crowd, especially if there's a big game on. (☎310-396-9250; www.stellabarra.com; 2000 Main St; salads $10-11, pizzas $13-16; ☺5pm-midnight Mon-Thu, 11am-1am Fri, from 10:30am Sat, 10:30am-11pm Sun)

Sunny Blue

JAPANESE $

18 Map p92, B7

A new *omusubi* joint and the first of its kind in LA. What is *omusubi* you ask? It's a Japanese sandwich-cum-handroll where fillings like chicken curry, albacore with diced cucumber, or miso beef are stuffed in rice balls wrapped in seaweed. Sides include edamame, sunomono and kimchi. They also serve tasty black-sesame frozen yogurt. (☎310-399-9030; www. sunnyblueinc.com; 2728 Main St; omusubi from $3)

Drinking

Basement Tavern
BAR

19 Map p92, B7

A creative speakeasy, housed in the basement of the Victorian, and our favorite well in Santa Monica. We love it for their craft cocktails, intimate booths, island bar and nightly live-music calendar that features blues, jazz, bluegrass and rock bands. It gets way too busy on weekends for our taste, however. (www.basementtavern.com; 2640 Main St; ⏱5pm-2am)

Local Life
Santa Monica Markets

You haven't really experienced Santa Monica until you've explored one of the weekly outdoor farmers markets stocked with organic fruits, vegetables, flowers, baked goods and freshly shucked oysters. The Wednesday and Saturday **market** (Map 92, B3; www.smgov.net/portals/farmersmarket; 3rd & Arizona; ⏱9am-1pm Wed & Sat) is the biggest and arguably the best for fresh produce in all of LA, which is why it's so often patrolled by local chefs, but the **Sunday morning market** (Map 92, B7; 2612 Main St; ⏱9am-1pm Sun) is more of a community scene with live music, pony rides, a half-dozen cooked-food stalls and a bicycle valet (um, yes, we know, but it is free). Relax with the locals on the luscious green lawn.

Galley
STEAKHOUSE

20 Map p92, B7

A long-running and much beloved steak and seafood house has occupied this boat-themed restaurant since 1934 and we love the bar here. It's strung with Christmas lights, staffed by no-nonsense but fun barkeeps and is almost always packed with regulars. This is old Santa Monica, folks. (www.thegalleyrestaurant.net; 2442 Main St; ⏱5-11pm Mon-Sat, to 1am Sun)

Copa d'Oro
BAR

21 Map p92, B4

The cocktail menu was created by the talented Vincenzo Marianella – a man who knows his spirits, and has trained a team to concoct addictive cocktails from a well of top-end liquor and a produce bin of fresh herbs, fruits, juices and a few veggies, too. The rock tunes and the smooth, dark ambience don't hurt. (www.copadoro.com; 217 Broadway Ave; ⏱5:30pm-midnight Mon-Wed, to 2am Thu-Sat)

Bar Chloe
LOUNGE

22 Map p92, B4

Dark and elegant with dangling chandeliers, twinkling candles, intimate booths, crisp white tablecloths, and a Chamomile Mai Tai that has earned rave reviews. We wouldn't know, we ordered a whiskey neat. The tapas and sliders are decent, too. (www.barchloe.com; 1449 2nd St; ⏱6pm-midnight Mon, to 1am Tue, to 2am Wed-Fri, 7pm-2am Sat)

Chez Jay

BAR

23 🍺 Map p92, B5

Rocking since 1959, here's another nautical-themed dive that's dark and dank and all the more glorious for it. The food's not bad either. (www.chezjays. com; 1657 Ocean Ave; ⏱2pm-midnight Mon, 11:30am-2am Tue-Fri, 9am-2am Sat & Sun)

Zanzibar

CLUB

24 🍺 Map p92, B3

Beat freaks will be in heaven at this groovetastic den dressed in a sensuous Indian-African vibe with a shape-shifting global DJ lineup that goes from Arabic to Latin to African depending on the night. The crowd is just as multiculti. (www.zanzibarlive. com; 1301 5th St; cover $5-10; ⏱9pm-2am Tue-Sun)

Entertainment

Harvelle's

BLUES

25 ⭐ Map p92, B4

This blues grotto has been packing 'em in since 1931 but somehow still manages to feel like a well-kept secret. There are no big-name acts here, but the quality is usually high. Sunday's Toledo Show mixes soul, jazz and cabaret, and Wednesday night brings the always funky House of Vibe All-Stars. (☎310-395-1676; www.harvelles.com; 1432 4th St; cover $5-15)

McCabe's Guitar Shop

McCabe's Guitar Shop

LIVE MUSIC

26 ⭐ Map p92, E6

Sure, this mecca of musicianship sells guitars and other instruments, but you want to come for concerts in the back room or at their nearby **bar & grill** (2455 Santa Monica Blvd; ⏱11am-2am), where the likes of Jackson Browne, Charlie Hunter and Liz Phair have performed. (☎310-828-4497; www. mccabes.com; 3101 Pico Blvd; tickets $15-30)

Magicopolis

MAGIC

27 ⭐ Map p92, B4

You don't have to be an aspiring Harry Potter to enjoy the comedy-laced sleight-of-hand, levitation and other illusions performed by Steve Spills and cohorts in this intimate space. Escapes from reality last about 90 minutes, and there's even a small shop for all your wizard supplies. (☎310-451-2241; www. magicopolis.com; 1418 4th St; tickets $24-34; ⏰8pm Fri & Sat, 2pm Sat & Sun; 🎫)

Shopping

Planet Blue
FASHION

28 🔒 Map p92, B8

Everyone from moneyed hipsters to soccer moms to Hollywood royalty peruses the racks at this expansive and stylish boutique stocked with tremendous denim and contemporary casual

Local Life
Annenberg Community Beach House

Like a beach club for the rest of us, this sleek and attractive public **beach club** (Map 92, A1; www.beach house.smgov.net; 400 Pacific Coast Hwy; parking $3, swimming pool adult/senior/child $10/5/4; ⏰8:30am-5:30pm Nov-Mar, to 6:30pm Apr & Oct, to 8:30pm Jun-Sep), is built on actress Marion Davies' estate (she had a thing with William Randolph Hearst). It has a lap pool, lounge chairs, yoga classes, beach volleyball, a fitness room, photo exhibits and even poetry readings. There's a cafe nearby, and it's set on a sweet stretch of Santa Monica Beach.

collections, as well as high-end beauty essentials and some sexy silver, too. Men's gear can be found on **Montana Ave** (www.shopplanetblue.com; 800 14th St; ⏰10am-6pm). (www.shopplanetblue.com; 2940 Main St; ⏰10am-6pm)

Paris 1900
VINTAGE

29 🔒 Map p92, B7

An exquisite collection of vintage French fashion from 1900 to 1930, and a few new vintage-inspired garments. Expect the finest jewelry and lace with an emphasis on period bridal. Look for the Montmartre-inspired art-nouveau entry. (www.paris1900.com; 2703 Main St)

Aura Shop
NEW AGE

Well, you are in California. You may as well get your aura read. Yes, auras do exist (it's that heat energy radiating off your skin) and the color trails they leave behind signify...something, or so we're told. Just get the aura photo and the reading and believe it or not. Also sells books, candles and crystals. Near the Streetcraft Gallery (see 5 Map p92, B8; www.aurashop.com; 2914 Main St; ⏰11am-6pm Mon-Sat, to 5pm Sun)

Blues Jean Bar
DENIM

30 🔒 Map p92, D1

Belly up to the rustic wood bar and order yours by style (boot cut, skinny or straight), size and wash (dark, light, medium or distressed) and they'll find you something from their well of denim, which includes the likes of Henry and Bell, Fidelity, Hudson and more. Jeans range from $150 to $250. (📞855-341-0073; www.thebluesjeanbar.com; 1409 Montana Ave; 🕙10am-6pm Mon-Sat, 11am-5pm Sun)

Hundreds   URBAN

31 🔒 Map p92, B4

A 10-year-old LA-based, urban skate culture and hip-hop-inspired label with tailored T-shirts, hoodies, sweaters and jackets. It's all stylish and affordable. Lately they've collaborated with the artist James Jean, whose work graces some of their tees and skateboards. The boards are especially cool. They'll fully construct any of their decks for $135. (www.thehundreds.com; 416 Broadway Ave; 🕙11am-7pm Mon-Sat, noon-6pm Sun)

Third Street Promenade   MALL

32 🔒 Map p92, B3

Stretching for three long blocks, it offers carefree and car-free strolling and shopping accompanied by the sound of flamenco guitar or hip-hop acrobatics courtesy of street performers. (3rd St btwn Wilshire & Broadway)

Santa Monica Place   MALL

33 🔒 Map p92, B4

The mall at the south end of the Promenade is considerably posher than elsewhere along the strip. Think All Saints, Juicy Couture, Bloomingdales and Nordstrom, Michael Kors, and there's a Nike flagship too, along with epic views from the dining deck. (www.santamonicaplace.com; 395 Santa Monica Pl;

🕙10am-9pm Mon-Thu, to 10pm Fri & Sat, 11am-8pm Sun)

Hennessey & Ingalls   BOOKS

34 🔒 Map p92, B3

LA's best art and architecture bookstore features work from Matisse, Renzo Piano and all the giants of architecture, as well as lesser-known volumes on sustainable design and graffiti. All in a cavernous yet spare warehouse space with exposed beams and patrolled by staff who have forgotten more about design than most will ever know. (📞310-458-9074; www.hennesseyingalls.com; 214 Wilshire Blvd; 🕙10am-8pm)

Undefeated   SHOES

35 🔒 Map p92, B7

Get your kicks at this slammin' sneaker store specializing in vintage and limited editions, hand selected from the manufacturer by the manager. When new shipments arrive, expect sidewalk campouts. (www.undeftd.com; 2654b Main St; 🕙10am-7pm Mon-Sat, 11am-6pm Sun)

Fred Segal   FASHION, JEWELRY

36 🔒 Map p92, C4

Celebs and beautiful people circle this impossibly chic but slightly snooty warren of high-end boutiques, which straddles 5th St and dominates an entire block. (www.fredsegal.com; 500 Broadway; 🕙10am-7pm Mon-Sat, noon-6pm Sun)

Top Sights
Malibu

Getting There

🚗 The I-10 becomes the California Hwy 1 north in Santa Monica. Follow it to paradise.

🚌 MTA's Malibu Express line 534 leaves from Fairfax Ave and Washington Blvd.

Everyone needs a little Malibu. Here's a moneyed, stylish yet laid-back beach town and celebrity enclave that rambles for 27 miles along the Pacific Coast Hwy, blessed with the stunning natural beauty of its coastal mountains, pristine coves, wide sweeps of golden sand and epic waves. Lucky for you, it's all just a drive away.

Malibu at sunset

Don't Miss

Explore the Getty Villa

Getty Villa (☎310-430-7300; www.getty.edu; 17985 Pacific Coast Hwy; admission free; ⏰10am-5pm Wed-Mon; P) is an original Getty Museum set in a replica 1st-century Roman villa, and is a stunning 64-acre showcase for exquisite Greek, Roman and Etruscan antiquities amassed (legally and otherwise) by oil tycoon J Paul Getty.

El Matador State Beach

Arguably Malibu's most stunning beach, El Matador is where sandstone rock towers rise from emerald coves, topless sunbathers stroll through the tides, and dolphins breech the surface beyond the waves.

Get Barefoot on Zuma & Westward Beach

Zuma (30000 Pacific Coast Hwy; P; ◻MTA 534) owns a blonde sweep of sand that has been attracting valley kids to the shore since the 1970s, but we prefer adjacent **Westward Beach** (6800 Westward Rd; P; ◻MTA 534), where rip currents can be strong but the water is crystal clear much of the year and migrating whales buzz the break.

Ride the Swell at Surfrider Beach

Surf punks descend in droves to a point that shapes tasty waves. There are several breaks at Surfrider. The closest is well formed for beginners; the others demand short boards and advanced-level skill.

Cruise Cross Creek

Across from Surfrider Beach, the high-end mall Malibu Country Mart spans both sides of Cross Creek Rd.

☑ Top Tips

▶ It's best to explore Malibu midweek, especially in summer. That way you'll have the roads and the beaches mostly to yourself.

▶ Malibu is an ideal family destination. Kids can get busy getting dirty on the beach or in the hills, and mom can shop and celebrity-spot in the swanky shops off Cross Creek Rd.

▶ Parking on the PCH is free, and same goes for the road that links Zuma with Westward Beach, but if you park in a self-pay lot, make sure you pony up the cash or you will earn a $60 fine.

✖ Take a Break

A Malibu favorite, **Café Habana** (☎310-317-0300; www.habana-malibu.com; 3939 Cross Creek Rd; mains $14-22; ⏰11am-11pm Sun-Wed, to 1am Thu-Sat; P♿) does tacos, burritos and some Cuban classics like *ropa vieja* (shredded beef) and a pulled-pork sandwich.

Explore

Venice

If you were born too late, and have always been a little jealous of the hippie heyday, come down to the boardwalk and inhale an incense-scented whiff of Venice, a boho beach town and long-time haven for artists, New Agers, road-weary tramps, freaks and free spirits.

The Sights in a Day

☼ Line up with the disheveled masses at **Intelligentsia** (p113), for what is arguably the best morning Joe in town. Sip it slowly as you stroll **Abbot Kinney Blvd** (p109), stepping into shops and galleries and becoming one with the artsy, boho vibe.

☼ The prix-fixe lunch at **Joe's** (p110) is too good to ignore. Afterward, wander the **Venice Canals** (p109) before heading for the **Venice Boardwalk** (p106) where you can watch the muscle heads get pumped at **Muscle Beach** (p107), spy **graffiti** (p107) and watch the groms tear it up at the **skate park** (p107).

☾ After nightfall head to Rose Ave, where you can sip wine and nosh on charcuterie at **Venice Beach Wines** (p113), or opt for killer cocktails and sensational pasta at **Tasting Kitchen** (p110). Then double back to Abbot Kinney, especially if it's a **First Friday** (p115) night, or even if it's a plain old Sunday or Monday when **Hal's** (p113) offers free live jazz.

 Top Sights

Venice Boardwalk (p106)

 Best of Los Angeles

Eating
Tasting Kitchen (p110)

Drinking
Venice Beach Wines (p113)

Shopping
Abbot Kinney Blvd (p109)

Getting There

🚌 **Bus** MTA, LA's principal transit authority, connects Venice with most other parts of town. Santa Monica's Big Blue Bus connects Venice with Santa Monica.

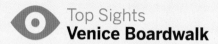

Top Sights
Venice Boardwalk

Life in Venice moves to a different rhythm, and nowhere more so than on the famous Venice Boardwalk, officially known as Ocean Front Walk. It's a freak show, a human zoo, a twisted carnival, but as far as LA experiences go, it's a must. Encounters with budding Schwarzeneggers, hoop dreamers, a Speedo-clad snake charmer and a roller-skating Sikh minstrel jamming like Hendrix are almost guaranteed.

👁 Map p108, A3

Venice Pier to Rose Ave

🕐 24hr

Venice Boardwalk

Don't Miss

Venice Beach Skate Park

Local skate punks have shredded the Boardwalk for generations, but one particular patch of concrete has now been officially molded into the steel-fringed **Venice Beach Skate Park** (1800 Ocean Front Walk; ☉dawn-dusk). Expect 17,000 sq ft of vert, tranny and street terrain with unbroken ocean views. The old-school-style skate run and the world-class pool lure spectators.

Muscle Beach

Gym rats with an exhibitionist streak can get a tan and a workout at **Muscle Beach** (www.musclebeach.net; 1800 Ocean Front Walk; per day $10; ☉8am-7pm May-Sep, to 6pm Oct-Apr), the famous outdoor gym right on the boardwalk where Arnold once bulked up.

Graffiti Park

Venice Beach has long been associated with street art, and for decades there was a struggle between outlaw artists and law enforcement. Art won out and now the **Venice Beach Graffiti Park** (1800 Ocean Front Walk; ☉dawn-dusk), a conglomeration of tagged-up towers and a free standing concrete wall near the skate park, is forever open to aerosol Picassos.

☑ Top Tips

▶ During the summer the Boardwalk is always alive. Off-season, there is still life around sunset when crowds gather at cafes, bars and on the bike path.

▶ The Sunday-afternoon drum circle draws hundreds of revelers for tribal jamming and spontaneous dancing on the grassy mounds beyond the skate park.

▶ South of the Venice Pier at Washington Blvd, the throng dissipates and the golden sands unfurl in a more pristine manner. Waves roll in consistently and are ideal for body surfing, and volleyball games tend to erupt at a moment's notice.

✗ Take a Break

If you're in need of a psychic shower, head to the groovy cafes and galleries on upscale, yet still boho, Abbot Kinney Blvd.

0   400 m
0   0.2 miles

3rd St
4th St
7th Ave
Lincoln Blvd

Rose Ave

Sunset Ave

Vernon Ave

Indiana Ave

Brooks Ave

Broadway St

Westminster Ave

San Juan Ave

Santa Clara Ave

California Ave

Pacific Ave

Main St

2nd St

5th Ave

Ocean Front Walk

Speedway

Abbot Kinney Boulevard

Abbot Kinney Blvd

Electric Ave

Santa Monica State Beach

Venice Beach

Venice Boardwalk

Westminster Ave

San Juan Ave

Market St

Windward Ave

VENICE

Venice Way

Grand Blvd

Mildred Ave

Dell Ave

LA Louver

N Venice Blvd

S Venice Blvd

Venice Canals

Canal Park

Venice Canals

Santa Monica Bay

South Venice Beach

Speedway

Dell Ave

Venice Way

Abbot Kinney Blvd

Washington Blvd

For reviews see

◎	Top Sights	p106
◎	Sights	p109
✕	Eating	p109
🍸	Drinking	p113
★	Entertainment	p114
🔒	Shopping	p114

Sights

Abbot Kinney Boulevard
SHOPPING DISTRICT

1  Map p108, B2

The impossibly hip and beautiful mile-long stretch of Abbot Kinney Blvd between Venice Blvd and Main St is chock-a-block with unique boutiques, galleries, lofts, vintage clothing stores and sensational restaurants.

LA Louver
GALLERY

2 Map p108, A4

The best art gallery in Venice, and arguably the best in the entire city, LA Louver was established by Peter Gouls in 1975, and since 1994 has been housed in a landmark building designed by Frederick Fisher. A contemporary art gallery, it features rotating, museum-quality exhibitions that show for five to six weeks. (www.lalouver.com; 45 N Venice Blvd; admission free; ⊘10am-6pm Tue-Sat)

Venice Canals
NEIGHBORHOOD

3 Map p108, B5

Even many Angelenos have no idea that just a couple of blocks away from the Boardwalk madness is an idyllic neighborhood that preserves 3 miles of Kinney's canals. The **Venice Canal Walk** threads past eclectic homes, over bridges and waterways where ducks preen and locals lolly gag in little rowboats. It's best accessed from either Venice or Washington Blvds.

WENDY CONNETT/GETTY IMAGES ©

Venice Canals

Eating

Gjelina
ITALIAN $$$

4 Map p108, C4

Carve out a slip on the communal table between the hipsters and yuppies, or get your own slab of wood on the elegant, tented stone terrace, and dine on imaginative small plates (raw yellowtail spiced with chili and mint and drenched in olive oil and blood orange), and sensational thin-crust, wood-fired pizza. They serve until midnight. (☎310-450-1429; www.gjelina.com; 1429 Abbot Kinney Blvd; dishes $8-26; ⊘11:30am-midnight Mon-Fri, from 9am Sat & Sun; 🚶)

Understand
Art is All Around Us

Who needs galleries when you've got outdoor art? Just ask Jonathan Borofsky's 30ft sad-faced ballerina clown at the corner of Main St and Rose Ave. Or walk one block south to ponder Claes Oldenburg and Coosje van Bruggen's massive binoculars, flanking the Frank Gehry–designed Chiat/Day building. As for murals, Venice has a plethora, so be sure to look up while you walk. Along Ocean Front Walk, check out Rip Cronk's *Venice Reconstituted* and *Homage to a Starry Night,* a tribute to Vincent Van Gogh.

Tasting Kitchen   ITALIAN $$$

5 Map p108, C4

From the salt-roasted branzino to the porcini-crusted hanger steak to the burger and the quail, it's all very good here. Especially the pastas (that bucatini is a gift from the gods), and the cocktails, of course. Which is why it's almost always packed. Book ahead. (310-392-6644; www.thetastingkitchen. com; 1633 Abbot Kinney Blvd; mains $16-40; 10:30am-2pm Sat & Sun, 6pm-late daily)

Scopa   ITALIAN $$$

6 Map p108, D5

Venice cool has leaked into the Marina Del Rey border regions with wonderful results. This place is big and open with polished concrete floors and an expansive marble L-shaped bar. The crudo bar serves scallops and steak tartare, four varieties of oysters, uni and mussels, while mains include a whole roasted branzino and a 24oz T-bone. (310-821-1100; www.scopaital ianroots.com; 2905 Washington Blvd; dishes $6-49; 5pm-2am)

Superba   NEW AMERICAN $$

7 Map p108, C1

A sleek glass box of culinary goodness, this is where you order plentiful small plates and pastas and dine family style. Start with one of their toasts – braised bacon and tomato marmalade perhaps? Move onto fried chicken in a red-wine vinegar glaze or the ocean trout crudo, and finish with a pasta. (310-399-6400; www.superba snackbar.com; 533 Rose Ave; dishes $8-19; 10:30am-2:30pm Fri-Sun, 6-10:30pm Sun-Thu, 6-11:30pm Fri & Sat)

Joe's   CALIFORNIAN, FRENCH $$$

8 Map p108, B2

Joe's was one of the first restaurants on Abbot Kinney's restaurant row and, like a fine wine, only seems to get better with age. It's casual yet stylish with gimmick-free Cal-French food. The best deal here is the three-course, prix-fixe lunch for $19. No cell phones allowed! (310-399-5811; www.joes restaurant.com; 1023 Abbot Kinney Blvd; mains $10-32; noon-2:30pm & 6-10pm Tue-Fri, from 11am Sat & Sun; P)

Axe

ASIAN FUSION $$

9 Map p108, B2

One of our favorite kitchens in Venice offers light, healthy and tasty Asian fusion. At lunch get the basic bowl, which combines brown rice, marinated cucumber, sprouts and other veggies with grilled chicken, salmon or tofu. At dinner they do a range of seafood mains, braised rabbit and delicious housemade pork sausage served in chic, minimalist environs. (☏310-664-9787; www. axerestaurant.com; 1009 Abbot Kinney Blvd; mains $12-24; ☷9am-11am & 11:30am-3pm Wed-Fri, 6-10pm Wed & Thu, 6-10:30pm Fri & Sat, 6-9:30pm Sun; P)

Abbot's Pizza Company

PIZZA $

10 Map p108, C3

Join the flip-flop crowd at this shoebox-sized pizza kitchen for habit-forming bagel-crust pies tastily decorated with tequila-lime chicken, portobello mushrooms, goat cheese and other gourmet morsels served up at tummy-grumbling speed. (☏310-396-7334; www.abbotspizzaco.com; 1407 Abbot Kinney Blvd; slices $3-5, pizzas $12-29; ☷11am-11pm Sun-Thu, to midnight Fri & Sat)

Lemonade

CALIFORNIAN $

11  Map p108, C4

The first incarnation of an imaginative, local-market cafe with a lineup of tasty salads (think watermelon radish and chili or tamarind pork and spicy carrots), stockpots

Abbot's Pizza Company

bubbling with lamb and stewed figs or miso-braised short ribs, and it has six kinds of lemonade augmented with blueberries and mint or watermelon and rosemary. It serves up yummy sweets, too. (http://lemonadela.com; 1661 Abbot Kinney Blvd; meals $8-13; ☷11am-9pm)

Oscar's Cerveteca

MEXICAN FUSION $$

12 Map p108, C1

A gourmet Mexican kitchen with fusion digressions (like the chorizo burger and the mac 'n' cheese with bacon). The patio is inviting, but so is the stylish interior, with that wide marble bar, craftsman drafts (this is a *cerveteca*, or beer bar, after all), and global tunes on the sound system. (www.cervetecala.com; 523 Rose Ave; mains $12-21; ⏱5-11pm Mon-Thu, 5pm-midnight Fri, 2pm-midnight Sat, 2-11pm Sun)

Wurstkuche
SAUSAGE $

13 Map p108, D2

Set in a brick-house loft, but sealed off from the on-rushing madness of Lincoln Blvd, this German sausage and beer *haus* specializes in three things: gourmet and classic grilled sausages; fine Belgian, German and North American beers; and Belgian fries with ample dipping sauces. (www.wurstkuche.com; 625 Lincoln Blvd; dishes $4-8; ⏱11am-midnight, bar to 2am)

Fig Tree's Café
CALIFORNIAN $$

14 Map p108, A1

The best eats on the Boardwalk. Here you can munch shitake omelettes made with organic eggs, ginger noodles, or a pesto-brushed, arugula-dressed salmon sandwich. The veg-heads will appreciate the spinach nut burger. Meals come with complimentary sea views. (www.figtreescafe.com; 429 Ocean Front Walk; appetizers $8-11, mains $12-16; ⏱8am-8pm;)

Pork Belly's
BARBECUE $

15 Map p108, C3

It's always been a BBQ joint, but it's been reimagined in the kind of place that serves new-school chopped chicken and brisket sandwiches, and a slow-smoked pork belly topped with BBQ sauce or in a stripped down BLT sandwich on sourdough with aioli. They also fry pickles and serve sweet potato tots. (☎424-777-8875; www.pork-bellysla.com; 1146 Abbot Kinney Blvd; mains $9-14; ⏱11am-9pm)

Gratitude Cafe
VEGETARIAN $$

16 Map p108, C1

The menu is dotted with affirmations like Magical (that's a housemade veggie burger), Gracious (a seasonal grain salad), Pure (a marinated kale salad), and Whole (a bowl of macrobiotic sea vegetables, braised yams, adzuki beans, sautéed kale and marinated kimchi). We'd roll our eyes too if the portions weren't so huge and they didn't have such a succulent coconut cream pie. (☎424-231-8000; cafegratitude venice.com; 512 Rose Ave; mains $10-14; ⏱8am-10pm Sun-Thu, to 11pm Fri & Sat)

Casa Linda
MEXICAN $

17 Map p108, C3

Consider the chicken mole plate, contemplate the tacos and tamales, then order an authentic *torta* (Mexican sandwich), smeared with black bean paste, and piled with avocado, onions and your choice of chicken, pork or tongue. The best part is it's affordable, which is saying something on this boulevard. (www.casalinda mexicangrill.com; 1357 Abbot Kinney Blvd; mains $6-10; ⏱11:30am-9:30pm)

Drinking

Venice Beach Wines   WINE BAR

A sweet and cozy hideaway, near Oscar's Cerveteca (see 12 Map p108, C1), with louvered benches and tables so close together you'll commune with strangers. Sip international wines by the glass or bottle (including a complex and invigorating French Syrah) and munch charcuterie, *pizzettas* and the like. For dessert try the *pot de crème*: it's 75% cacao and 100% orgasmic. (www.venicebeachwines.com; 529 Rose Ave; ⏰4-11pm Mon-Thu, to midnight Fri, 10:30am-midnight Sat, to 11pm Sun)

Townhouse & Delmonte Speakeasy   BAR

18 🍷 Map p108, A3

Upstairs is a cool, dark and perfectly dingy bar with pool tables, booths and good booze. Downstairs is the speakeasy, where DJs spin pop, funk and electronic music, comics take the mic and jazz players set up and jam. It's a reliably good time almost any night. (www.townhousevenice.com; 52 Windward Ave; ⏰5pm-2am Mon-Thu, noon-2am Fri-Sun)

Hal's Bar & Grill   BAR

19 🍷 Map p108, C3

The name may evoke brass and wood, but Hal's dining room is an industrial loft brightened by revolving art and buzzing with locals who treat the place like an extended living room. They have free live jazz on Sunday and Monday. (☎310-396-3105; www.halsbarandgrill.com; 1349 Abbot Kinney Blvd)

Brig   BAR

20 🍷 Map p108, D4

Old-timers remember this place as a pool hall dive owned by ex-boxer Babe Brandelli (that's him and his wife on the outside mural). Now it's a bit sleeker, and attracts a trendy mix of grown-up beach bums, arty professionals and professional artists. On First Fridays, the parking lot attracts a fleet of LA's famed food trucks. (www.thebrig.com; 1515 Abbot Kinney Blvd; ⏰6pm-2am)

Intelligentsia Coffeebar   CAFE

In this hip, industrial, minimalist monument to the coffee gods, skilled baristas – who roam the circle bar and command more steaming machines than seems reasonable – never short you on foam or caffeine, and the Cake Monkey scones and muffins are addictive. Find Hal's Bar & Grill (see 19 🍷 Map p108, C3) and you're nearly there. (www.intelligentsiacoffee.com; 1331 Abbot Kinney Blvd; ⏰6am-8pm Mon-Wed, 6am-11pm Thu & Fri, 7am-11pm Sat, 7am-8pm Sun; 📶)

Tom's   CAFE

21 🍷 Map p108, C3

You know Tom, the one-for-one entrepreneur who made his name selling fun, slip-on canvas shoes and giving a pair away to underprivileged kids overseas for each one he sells in the States. Now he's doing the same with shades

DEEDEE DEGELIA/GETTY IMAGES ©

Strange Invisible perfumery

and coffee. His flagship store includes a wonderful back patio area that's wired with wi-fi. (www.toms.com; 1344 Abbot Kinney Blvd; ⊙6am-8pm Mon-Fri, 7am-9pm Sat, 7am-8pm Sun; 🛜)

Entertainment

Venice Beach Freakshow
SIDESHOW

22 ⭐ Map p108, A2

Here's a circus-style sideshow, including a live 20-minute show with a fire eater, a Rubber Girl and an Electric Lady who gets shot up with 100,000 volts of electricity with nary a twitch. There's also a gallery with 60 of the strangest creatures on earth, including 10 two-headed animals. (☎310-314-1808; www.venicebeachfreakshow.com; 909 Ocean Front Walk; admission $5; ⊙10am-6pm Sat & Sun)

Shopping

A + R Store
GIFTS

23 🔒 Map p108, C3

This is top-end industrial design and a great browse, with interesting ceramic speakers, ergonomic headphones, chairs, wooden toys and strange-yet-alluring high-format cameras. (☎800-913-0071; www.aplusrstore.com; 1121 Abbot Kinney Blvd; ⊙11am-7pm Tue-Sun)

Alternative
CLOTHING

Alternative, close to Hal's Bar & Grill (see 19 🍴 Map p108, C3), built its name on organic cotton and recycled poly hoodies and tees, but has expanded its collection to include beachy flannels, cardigans, skirts and slacks. (www.alternativeapparel.com; 1337 Abbot Kinney Blvd; ⊙11am-7pm)

Will
LEATHER GOODS

24 🔒 Map p108, C3

A terrific leather-goods store out of Portland, and one of just three nationwide. They do fine leather bags, briefcases, backpacks, belts, wallets and sandals for men and women. Our favorite was the bike messenger bag inlaid with colorful remnant Oaxacan wool. (www.willleathergoods.com; 1360 Abbot Kinney Blvd; ⊙10am-8pm)

Nightcap
LACE

25 Map p108, C3

A branded store from a locally designed and made label known for their stretch lace, a material sourced from French and Italian textiles. They started with loungewear, so you know it's comfortable, then transitioned into a full ready-to-wear line. Every girl needs a nice black dress, and they have a lace variety that really is something special. (https://nightcapclothing. com; 1225 Abbot Kinney Blvd; ⏰11am-6pm Tue-Sat, from noon Sun)

Arbor
SKATEBOARDS

26 Map p108, A1

A Venice homegrown label since 1995, they started on Lincoln Blvd as a snowboard shop. The snowboards have since moved to a new **shop** (www. arborcollective.com; 102 Washington Blvd; ⏰11am-7pm) south of the Venice pier. This skate shop is on the north end. In addition to decks they sell chinos, hoodies and T-shirts. (www.arborcollec tive.com; 305 Ocean Front Walk; ⏰11am-7pm)

Alexis Bittar
JEWELRY

27 Map p108, C4

High-end jewelry known for Bittar's use of lucite, which is handcarved and painted in his Brooklyn studio. Some of it looks like stone. He started by selling it on the streets in Manhattan, where he was picked up by the MOMA store. (☎310-452-6901; www.alexisbittar. com; 1612 Abbot Kinney Blvd; ⏰11am-7pm Mon-Sat, noon-6pm Sun)

Top Tip

Walk this Way

Abbot Kinney Blvd is frequently celebrating...something. In late September, the **Abbot Kinney Festival** (www.abbotkinney.org) draws thousands of revelers, as does the now institutionalized **First Friday** (www.abbotkinney1stfridays.com) art walks, when the galleries and shops stay open late and you can roam all night with the tramps, hippies, weirdos, fashionistas, yuppies, hotties and squares.

Strange Invisible
APOTHECARY

28 Map p108, B3

Organic perfumes crafted from wild and natural ingredients and blended into intoxicating perfumes with names like Aquarian Rose and Fair Verona, although some are gender neutral. It also sells dark chocolate. (☎310-314-1505; www.siperfumes.com; 1138 Abbot Kinney Blvd; ⏰11am-7pm Mon-Sat, noon-6pm Sun)

Warakuku
SHOES, FASHION

29 Map p108, C3

Warakuku is a compact Japanese-owned shop for shoe lovers. It blends Far East couture with mainstream street brands such as Puma and Converse. Some 60% of the shoes are imported from Japan, the rest are domestic limited editions. (www. warakukuusa.com; 1225 Abbot Kinney Blvd; ⏰10am-7pm)

Local Life
Manhattan Beach, Beyond the Sand

A bastion of surf music and the birthplace of beach volleyball, Manhattan Beach may have gone chic, but that salty-dog heart still beats. Yes, the downtown area along Manhattan Beach Blvd has seen an explosion of trendy restaurants and boutiques, but the real action is beach-side, where the bikinis are small, the waves kind and the smiles are over-sized as those sunglasses.

Getting There

🚗 Two exits off I-405 serve Manhattan Beach, including Rosecrans Blvd and Inglewood Ave, which merges with Manhattan Beach Blvd.

🚌 MTA 109

❶ Sweat & Tumble at Sand Dune Park

Sand Dune Park (www.citymb.info; cnr 33rd & Bell Ave; ⏰6am-9pm Apr-Oct, 6am-8pm Nov-Mar; 🚻) requires reservations if you wish to access the long, deep 100ft-high natural sand dune. Adults enjoy their requisite running/suffering here. The kids will love hurling themselves down the dune again and again.

❷ Uncle Bill's Pancake House

Sexy surfers, tottering toddlers and gabbing girlfriends – everybody comes to **Uncle Bill's** (📞310-545-5177; www.unclebills.net; 1305 N Highland Ave; dishes $8-15; ⏰6am-3pm Mon-Fri, from 7am Sat & Sun; 🚻) for the famous pancakes and big fat omelettes.

❸ Photo Bomb

No surf, sport or music nut should miss the dazzling work on display at **Bo Bridges Photography** (📞310-937-3764; www.bobridgesgallery.com; 112 Manhattan Ave; ⏰11am-5pm Sat & Sun, varies Mon-Fri). Bridges made his name in the water shooting the likes of Kelly Slater at Pipeline, and parlayed that into mainstream sport and pop culture success. You'll see plenty of famous faces on the wall.

❹ Hit the Beach

Ditch the shoes on this wide sweep of golden sand, where you'll find pick-up volleyball courts, a pier with breathtaking blue sea views from the edge, consistent sandy bottom surf and a giddy, pretty population that still can't believe they get to live here.

❺ MB Post

Trendy but friendly and unvarnished, **MB Post** (📞310-545-5405; www.eatmbpost.com; 1142 Manhattan Ave; small plates $9-13, mains $11-39; ⏰5-10pm Mon-Thu, 11:30am-10:30pm Fri, 10am-10:30pm Sat, 10am-10pm Sun; 🚻) offers globally inspired tapas. Walk in and dine at the long communal tables in the bar, or make a reservation and get close at a small table in the dining room.

❻ Indulge Your Ice Cream Addiction

There's a damn good reason the hordes are lined up along the wall and out the door of **Manhattan Beach Creamery** (www.mbcreamery.com; 1120 Manhattan Ave; ice cream $4-6; ⏰10am-10pm Sun-Thu, to 11pm Fri & Sat). It's for gourmet housemade creams, served in a cup, cone or smashed between two freshly baked chocolate-chip cookies.

❼ Ercole's

A funky counterpoint to the HD-inundated, design-heavy sports bars on Manhattan Beach Blvd. **Ercole's** (📞310-372-1997; 1101 Manhattan Ave; ⏰10am-2am) is a dark, chipped, well-irrigated hole with a barn door open to everyone from salty barflies to yuppie pub crawlers to volleyball stars.

Explore

Downtown

Downtown Los Angeles has gone from derelict to fascinating in a decade. Here's stunning architecture from 19th-century Beaux Arts to futuristic Frank Gehry, world-class music, top-notch art, superb dining and sinful cocktails. It's a power nexus and a gritty hipster haven for indie artists and designers. Don't expect Manhattan, but the momentum is here, and now is the time to explore.

The Sights in a Day

☼ Have breakfast at **Eggslut** (p130) before meandering down Broadway past the old theaters to the **Fashion District** (p122), where even if there isn't a sample sale on you can explore the **California Market Center** (p123), and absorb the general fashionista vibe. Hit the epic **Grammy Museum** (p126) before heading north.

☼ Grab lunch among suits, designers and artists at **Bar Ama'** (p128) before strolling north past Pershing Square and into the Financial District. From here it's an easy walk two blocks north to the **Walt Disney Concert Hall** (p120), where you can catch the last tour of the day. Then walk southeast to the **Museum of Contemporary Art** (pictured left; p126) and the **Grand Central Market** (p126).

☽ If it's a summer Friday night, you can start your evening with free live music at the **California Plaza** (p127). Otherwise, head to the **Ace Hotel rooftop** (p133) for a sundowner, then head around the corner to **Woodspoon** (p129) for dinner and over to **Las Perlas** (p132) for a nightcap.

For a local's day in downtown see p122.

⦿ Top Sights

Walt Disney Concert Hall (p120)

◯ Local Life

Shopping the Fashion District (p122)

♥ Best of Los Angeles

Eating
Bar Ama' (p128)

Bestia (p130)

Sushi Gen (p131)

Woodspoon (p129)

Drinking
Las Perlas (p132)

Varnish (p131)

Sights
Grand Central Market (p126)

Grammy Museum (p126)

MOCA (p126)

Getting There

Ⓜ **Metro** Downtown is well connected to Hollywood by the Metro Red Line, while Metrolink connects downtown with Long Beach and Burbank.

🚌 **Bus** MTA connects downtown with all parts of town. Santa Monica's Big Blue Bus connects downtown with the shore.

Top Sights
Walt Disney Concert Hall

A molten blend of steel, music and psychedelic architecture, Frank Gehry pulled out all the stops for his iconic concert venue that's the home base of the Los Angeles Philharmonic, but also hosts contemporary bands such as Phoenix and classic jazz men such as Sonny Rollins. The building is a gravity-defying sculpture of heaving and billowing stainless-steel walls that conjure visions of a ship adrift in a rough sea.

◉ Map p124, E2

☎ info 213-972-7211, tickets 323-850-2000

www.laphil.org

111 S Grand Ave

admission free

🕑 guided tours usually 12pm & 1pm Tue-Sat

Don't Miss

Los Angeles Philharmonic

The only way to experience the auditorium is to buy tickets. The **Los Angeles Philharmonic** (☎323-850-2000; www.laphil.org) curates the calendar and, in addition to classical shows, it often hosts jazz luminaries. The room feels like the inside of a finely crafted cello, clad in walls of smooth Douglas fir. Even seats below the giant pipe organ offer excellent sight lines.

Red Cat

Red Cat (www.redcat.org; 631 W 2nd St), an acronym for Roy and Edna Disney/Cal Arts Theater, is the curious name of LA's most avante garde theater company, which is based in the Walt Disney Concert Hall complex. Admission to their art gallery, which rotates exhibitions every six weeks, is free.

Pipe Organ

The stunning pipe organ, a gift to LA county from the Toyota Corporation, incorporates 6134 pipes and took over 2000 hours to tune. The longest pipe is more than 32ft long and weighs upwards of 800 lbs. Shipped by sea from Germany, the instrument's total weight is over 40 metric tons. And it sounds just that big.

☑ Top Tips

▸ Self-guided tours narrated by John Lithgow are offered most days, but 60-minute docent-led tours may also be available. Consult the schedule online.

▸ To save money on parking, find a cheaper lot in Little Tokyo or the Jewelry District and walk.

▸ Tours do not include a glimpse of the auditorium, so the best way to experience the concert hall is to buy tickets and see a show.

✗ Take a Break

Little Tokyo is about six blocks away. If you're hungry, grab an epic udon bowl at **Marugame Monzo** (p131) or a sushi lunch at **Sushi Gen** (p131).

Local Life
The Fashion District

Bargain hunters love this frantic 100-block warren of fashion. Deals can be amazing, but first-timers are often bewildered by the district's size and immense selection. And by the sheer juxtaposition of sassy fashionistas in minis, knee-high boots and new-school cardigans wandering among drunks with neck tattoos and a perma-haze.

❶ Back to School

Technically it's a bit west of the district, but the **Fashion Institute of Design & Merchandising** (FIDM; www.fidm. edu; 919 S Grand Ave; ⏰10am-4pm Tue-Sat), a private college with an international student body, is very much part of its soul. The gallery has some interesting rotating exhibits, including costumes worn in Academy Award–nominated movies.

2 Sample Sales

Every last Friday of the month from 9am to 2pm, clued-in fashionistas descend upon the corner of 9th and Olympic armed with cash and attitude to catfight it out for designer clothes priced below wholesale. Their destinations: the showrooms at the **Gerry Building** (www.gerrybuilding.com; 910 S Los Angeles St), the **Cooper** (☏213-627-3754; www.cooperdesignspace.com; 860 S Los Angeles St) and the **New Mart** (☏213-627-0671; www.newmart.net; 127 E 9th St).

3 Bargain District

One of the most laid-back and festive corners of the district, there are over 150 shops and stalls crammed into this single laneway. **Santee Alley** (www.thesanteealley.com; Santee St & 12th St; ⊙9:30am-6pm) is known for its designer knockoffs.

4 Quick Fix

Need that quick fix to sate you through the sample-sale madness? Head to the **Market** (www.market restaurants.com; 862 S Los Angeles St; mains $9-12; ⊙8am-4pm Mon-Fri; ✏️♿) for a pressed Cuban (citrus-glazed pork, ham and manchego) or a seared-ahi and soba-noodle salad. Eat at common, brushed-metal tables with fellow shoppers and steely-eyed designers.

5 The Hub

Although it's no longer the hippest building in the district, the **California Market Center** (☏213-630-3600; www.californiamarketcenter.com; 110 E 9th St) remains its axis, and resident designers hold sample sales here.

6 Om Hour

Yoga does not get any louder or more effing fun than the variety you'll find at **Peace Yoga** (www.peaceyogagallery.com; 903 S Main St; per class $10-20), where Cheri Rae, the resident, foul-mouthed guru, has a local DTLA following based on her brash yet tender personality, her kick-ass classes and her yummy raw kitchen.

7 Clink of the Glass

A popular Fashion District well, **Pattern Bar** (www.patternbar.com; 100 W 9th St; ⊙noon-midnight Sun-Thu, to 2am Fri, 6pm-2am Sat; ☐MTA 66) comes with pebbled marble floors, vintage bar stools and a classic rock soundtrack. Cocktails are christened for fashion icons like DVF and McQueen, and it serves tapas and *arepas* (flatbreads).

8 Art for the People

A massive, mad swirl of art lovers invades downtown once a month for free, self-guided, liberally lubricated **Downtown Art Walks** (www.downtownart walk.org; admission free; ⊙noon-9pm 2nd Thu of month) that link more than 40 galleries and museums across the downtown grid. You'll find most between 3rd and 9th and Broadway and Main.

Chick Hearn Ct

Georgia St

A **B** **C** **D**

1

⭐ 29

Pasadena Fwy

Staples
Center

Cottage Pl

Francisco St

2 🔘
Grammy
Museum

S Figueroa St

S Flower St

**7th
St/Metro
Center**
Ⓜ

**ARCO
Plaza**

Macy's
Plaza

Maguire Gardens

Bank
Ameri
Plaza

2

W 12th St

S Hope St

W 11th St

**SOUTH
PARK**

Grand
Hope Park

S Grand Ave

W 7th St

S Grand Ave

California
Plaza

❌ 12 **FINANCIAL
DISTRICT**

S Olive St

Midway Pl

W Olympic Blvd

S 9th St

United
Artists
Theatre

S 8th St

S Hill St

S Broadway

9 🔘 ❓ 27

❓ 28

**JEWELRY
DISTRICT**

32 🔒

Pershing
Square

W 6th St

Ⓜ Pershing
Square

26

W 5th St

S Main St

⭐ 31

S Broadway

33
🔒

W 4th St

3

S Los Angeles St

California
Market
Center

❌ 13   25

S Spring St

❌ 5
17

🔒

20

Santee St

**FASHION
DISTRICT**

S Main St

Harlem Pl

34

11 ❌

Harlem Pl

Maple Ave

E 11th St

E 9th St

E 8th St

Flower
Market

S 7th St

E 6th St

21

E 5th St

14 ❌

Wall St

E Olympic Blvd

❌ 16 🍴 22

Winston St

4

San Julian St

San Julian St

E 3rd St

S San Pedro St

Crocker St

Agatha St

Towne Ave

Stanford Ave

5

❌ 15
▼

ARTS DISTRICT Ⓟ

E F G H

1 km
0.5 miles

N Beaydry Ave

1

W Temple St

Beverly Blvd

Pasadena Fwy

College St

W 1st St

N Figueroa St

2

Santa Ana Fwy

W Cesar E Chavez Ave

Alpine St

Walt Disney Concert Hall

Hope St

10

30

N Grand Ave

Alpine Park

Yale St

Museum of Contemporary Art

S Olive St

Civic Center

6

Cathedral of Our Lady of the Angels

8
Chinatown

W College St

3

W Temple St

CHINATOWN

tral ket

Civic Center/ Tom Bradley

N Hill St

N Broadway

Chinatown

3

Arcadia St

Old St

N Broadway

N Spring St

N Spring St

N Alameda St

N Main St

N Main St

5
Pueblo de Los Angeles

E 2nd St

N Los Angeles St

El Pueblo de Los Angeles

LITTLE TOKYO

Judge John Aiso St

4 *Union Station*

4

Japanese Village Plaza

19

Union Station/ Gateway Transit Center

Amtrak

E Cesar E Chavez Ave

N Alameda St

E Temple St

Metrolink Station

N Vignes St

Banning St

Santa Ana Fwy

E 1st St

5

23

N Vignes St

Sights

Grand Central Market
MARKET

1 ⊙ Map p124, D3

On the ground floor of a 1905 beaux arts building where architect Frank Lloyd Wright once kept an office. Stroll along the sawdust-sprinkled aisles beneath old-timey ceiling fans and neon signs, past stalls piled high with mangoes, peppers and jicamas, and glass bins filled with dried chilies and nuts. (www.grandcentralsquare.com; 317 S Broadway; ⊙9am-6pm)

Grammy Museum
MUSEUM

2 ⊙ Map p124, A1

The highlight of LA Live. Music lovers will get lost in interactive exhibits, which define, differentiate and link musical genres, while live footage strobes. You can glimpse such things as GnR's bass drum, Lester Young's tenor, Yo Yo Ma's cello and Michael's glove (though exhibits and collections do rotate). (www.grammymuseum.org; 800 W Olympic Blvd; adult/child $13/11, after 6pm $8; ⊙11:30am-7:30pm Mon-Fri, from 10am Sat & Sun; 📶)

Museum of Contemporary Art
MUSEUM

3 ⊙ Map p124, E2

A collection that arcs from the 1940s to the present and includes works by Mark Rothko, Dan Flavin, Joseph Cornell and other big-shot contemporary artists is housed in a postmodern building by Arata Isozaki. Galleries are below ground, yet brightened with skylights. (MOCA; 📞213-626-6222; www. moca.org; 250 S Grand Ave; adult/child $12/free, 5-8pm Thu free; ⊙11am-5pm Mon & Fri, to 8pm Thu, to 6pm Sat & Sun)

Union Station
LANDMARK

4 ⊙ Map p124, G4

Built on the site of LA's original Chinatown, the station opened in 1939 as America's last grand rail station. It's a glamorous exercise in Mission Revival with art deco accents. The marble-floored main hall, with cathedral ceilings, original leather chairs and grand chandeliers, is breathtaking. (www.amtrak.com; 800 N Alameda St; 🅿)

Pueblo de Los Angeles
MONUMENT

5 ⊙ Map p124, G4

LA was a full-blown community a good 100 years before DW Griffith showed up. Grab a map at restored Firehouse No 1 (the Plaza Firehouse) then wander through narrow Olvera St's vibrant Mexican-themed stalls. For LA's oldest building, see Avila Adobe then walk through the Sepulveda House and its visitor center to see a restored 1800s-era kitchen and bedroom. (📞213-628-1274; elpueblo.lacity. org; btwn Main & Alameda Sts; admission free; ⊙tour office 10am-3pm)

Grand Central Market

Cathedral of Our Lady of the Angels

CHURCH

6 ⊙ Map p124, F3

José Rafael Moneo mixed Gothic proportions with contemporary design for his 2002 Cathedral of Our Lady of the Angels, which exudes a calming serenity achieved by soft light filtering through its alabaster panes. Wall-sized tapestries as detailed as a Michelangelo fresco festoon the main nave. (☎213-680-5200; www.olacathedral.org; 555 W Temple St; admission free; ⊗6:30am-6pm Mon-Fri, from 9am Sat, from 7am Sun; P)

California Plaza

LANDMARK

7 ⊙ Map p124, D2

California Plaza hosts Grand Performances (www.grandperformances.org), one of the best free summer performance series. (350 S Grand Ave)

Chinatown

CULTURAL DISTRICT

8 ⊙ Map p124, G3

Walk north from El Pueblo and you'll breach the dragon gates. After being forced to make room for Union Station, the Chinese resettled a few blocks north along Hill St and Broadway. Chinatown is still the community's traditional hub, even though most Chinese Americans now live in the San Gabriel Valley. (www.chinatownla.com)

United Artists Theatre
THEATER

9 Map p124, B3

This gorgeous Spanish Gothic theater, with ornate stone work and stained glass, was built in 1927 and bank-rolled by bygone heavyweights Mary Pickford, Douglas Fairbanks and Charlie Chaplin. Once the second-tallest building in the city next to City Hall, the Ace Hotel recently restored it with passionate attention to detail and it now uses it to host modern dance shows and rock concerts. (☎213-623-3233; www.acehotel.com/losangeles/theatre; 929 S Broadway)

Broad
MUSEUM

10 Map p124, E2

Due to be completed in 2015, this new museum promises to be both an architectural marvel and a deep and nourishing well of modern art.

(www.thebroad.org; 221 S Grand Ave; admission free)

Eating

Bar Ama'
MEXICAN FUSION $$$

11 Map p124, D3

One of three exquisite downtown restaurants with profound Mexican influences offered by Josef Centeno. This one fries pig ears, braises short rib, and smothers enchiladas with mole sauce. Brussel sprouts are garnished with pickled red onions, and the roasted cauliflower and cilantro pesto, served with cashews and pine nuts, is a tremendous veggie choice. (☎213-687-8002; www.bar-ama.com; 118 W 4th St; dishes $8-25, dinners $32-36; ⏰11:30am-2:30pm & 5:30-11pm Mon-Thu, 11:30am-3pm & 5:30pm-midnight Fri, 11:30am-midnight Sat, to 10pm Sun)

Sushi chef in Little Tokyo

Q Sushi
SUSHI $$$

12  Map p124, C2

A slender wedge of exquisite sushi. This stunning dark-and-blonde-wood sushi bar is all *omakase* (chef's selection) all the time. Highlights include a blow-torched toro with chili paste, and a tender octopus that's been braised in sake and brown sugar for two to three hours. They even brew their own soy sauce. (☎213-225-6285; www.qsushila.com; 521 W 7th St; per person lunch/dinner $75/165)

Woodspoon
BRAZILIAN $$

13 Map p124, B3

We love it all: the hand-picked china, the vintage pyrex pots of black beans and rice, and the Brazilian owner-operator who still chefs it up in the back. Her pork ribs fall off the bone in a bath of grits and gravy. Her take on steak frites incorporates wedges of fried yucca and her pot pie put this place on the map. (☎213-629-1765; www.woodspoonla.com; 107 W 9th St; mains $11-20; ☺11am-2:45pm & 5-10pm Tue-Fri, noon-3pm & 6-11pm Sat, closed Sun)

Thai Street Food
THAI $

Well-prepared Thai street food is crafted from organic and free-range ingredients and quality oils in downtown's fabulous Grand Central Market (see 1 Map p124, D3). They always do three set meals: a BBQ chicken served with sticky rice and *som tom* (green papaya salad), a Hainan chicken served with garlic rice and chicken soup, and a beef Paneng with coconut rice. (317 S Broadway; meals $9-10; ⏲11am-6pm)

Baco Mercat

FUSION $$$

14 Map p124, D4

At lunch it's an upscale *torta* (Mexican sandwich) joint – think beef tongue schnitzel or lamb meatballs – but at dinner it's a Mexican-Asian fusion dynamo. Seafood dishes include squid stuffed with shrimp and pine nuts, and a popular yellowtail collar. They also do intriguing veggie dishes, including a crispy eggplant and baby yellow-beet salad. (📞213-687-8808; www.bacomercat.com; 408 S Main St; dinners $29-58)

Bestia

ITALIAN $$$

15 Map p124, B5

The most sought-after reservation in town can be found at this new and splashy Italian kitchen in the Arts District. There are tasty pizzas and pastas, roasted chops and whole fish, and squid-ink risotto stuffed with chunks of lobster, mussels, clams and calamari. A worthy splurge indeed. (📞213-514-5724; www.bestia.com; 2121 7th Pl; dishes $10-29; ⏲6-11pm Sun-Thu, to midnight Fri & Sat)

Cole's

BAR & GRILL $

16 Map p124, C4

A funky old basement tavern known for originating the French dip sandwich way back in 1908, when those things cost a nickel. You know the drill – French bread piled with sliced lamb, beef, turkey, pork or pastrami, served *au jus* (with gravy). (www.213nightlife.com/colesfrenchdip; 118 E 6th St; sandwiches $6-9; ⏲11am-10pm Sun-Wed, to 11pm Thu, to 1am Fri & Sat)

Eggslut

DINER $

A classic breakfast counter has been brought back to life at the Grand Central Market (see 1 Map p124, D3) by local foodie punks who, among other things, stuff housemade turkey sausage, eggs and mustard aioli in brioche, and make a dish known only as 'the slut': a coddled egg nestled on top of potato purée poached in a glass jar and served with a toasted crostini. (www.eggslut.com; Grand Central Market, 317 S Broadway; dishes $6-10; ⏲8am-4pm)

Gorbals

EASTERN EUROPEAN $$

17 Map p124, D3

An Eastern European tapas joint set in the old Alexandria Hotel lobby. Menu mainstays include duck latkes with apple sauce, bacon-wrapped matzo balls served with pink-hot horseradish mayo and boneless lamb neck roasted with Ethiopian spices. (📞213-488-3408; www.thegorbalsla.com; 216 5th St; dishes $6-30; ⏲lunch & dinner)

Sushi Gen
JAPANESE $$

18 Map p124, E5

Come early to grab a table, and know that they don't do the 'look at me' kind of rolls. This is a classic Japanese sushi spot where seven chefs stand behind the blonde wood bar, carving thick slabs of melt-in-your-mouth salmon, buttery toro and a wonderful Japanese snapper, among other staples. Their sashimi special at lunch ($18) is a steal. (213-617-0552; www.sushigen.org; 422 E 2nd St; sushi $11-21; 11:15am-2pm & 5:30-9:45pm)

Marugame Monzo
JAPANESE $

19 Map p124, E4

If you care to step up from ramen to udon, come to this special dark-wood udon emporium where they make their noodles fresh in the open kitchen. Appetizers include tempura-fried chicken skin and raw, sliced scallops dolloped with flying-fish roe. But the udon is what draws the raves. (www.facebook.com/marugamemonzo; 329 E 1st St; mains $7-12; 11:30am-2:30pm & 5-10pm)

Maccheroni Republic
ITALIAN $$

20 Map p124, D3

Tucked away on a still ungentrified corner is this gem with a lovely heated patio and tremendous Italian slow-cooked food. Don't miss the *polpettine di gamberi* (flattened ground shrimp cakes fried in olive oil) and their range of delicious housemade pastas. They don't have beer or wine, but you're welcome to bring your own. (213-346-9725; 332 S Broadway Ave; mains $10-14; 11:30am-3pm & 5:30-10pm Mon-Fri, 5:30-10pm Sat, 4:30-9pm Sun)

Nickel Diner
DINER $$

21 Map p124, C3

Named for the intersection of 5th and Main, termed 'the Nickel' by nearby skid-row residents who used to come to this corner for their daily meds, this kitschy red-vinyl joint reimagines American diner fare. Avocados are stuffed with quinoa salad. Burgers piled with poblano chilies, and don't sleep on the maple-glazed bacon donut. (213-623-8301; www.nickeldiner.com; 524 S Main St; mains $7-14; 8am-3:30pm Tue-Sun, 6-10pm Tue-Sat)

Drinking

Varnish
BAR

If you like your cocktails precision-prepared with the freshest ingredients, look no further than this intimate, speakeasy-style, wood-panelled hipster hangout, a regular top-finisher at Tales of the Cocktail, the annual nationwide competition. Aficionados recommend you ask for the bartender's choice. It's located in the back of Cole's (see 16 Map p124, C4) restaurant. (213-622-9999; 213nightlife.com/thevarnish; 118 E 6th St; 7pm-2am)

View of downtown from a rooftop bar

Las Perlas

BAR

22 Map p124, C4

With Old Mexico whimsy, a chalkboard menu of over 80 tequilas and mescals, and friendly barkeeps who mix things like egg whites, blackberries and port syrup into new-school takes on the classic margarita, there's a reason we love downtown's best tequila bar. But if you truly want to dig tequila, select a highland variety and sip it neat. (107 E 6th St; ⏰7pm-2am Mon-Sat, 8pm-2am Sun)

Association

BAR

This hip basement bar flashes old-school glamour with leather bar stools and lounges tucked into intimate coves. But the bar is the thing. We're talking dozens of whiskeys, ryes, rums and tequilas. Find it close to Cole's (see 16 ⊗ Map p124, C4) restaurant. (www.theassociation-la.com; 110 E 6th St; ⏰7pm-2am)

One-Eyed Gypsy

BAR

23 Map p124, F5

Set just off the Little Tokyo swirl, this oh-so-dark carnival-themed joint comes with 10 craft beers on tap, peaked Arabic arches, a ski-ball arcade-game concession, a stage blessed with a circus curtain and live music nightly. Oh, and it serves a deep-fried Chocodile. Hence the hipster following. (www.one-eyedgypsy.com; 901 E 1st St; ⏱6pm-2am Wed-Sat)

Wolf & Crane BAR

24 Map p124, E5

A fun, new Little Tokyo bar with waxed concrete floors, a blonde-wood slab bar, common tables and built-in bench seating. They have flat screens for the ball games, Japanese art on the walls and nine locally crafted draught beers. But we prefer the house special, Wolf & Crane: a shot of Johnnie Red and a Sapporo. (☑213-935-8249; www.wolfandcranebar.com; 366 E 2nd St; ⏱5pm-2am Mon-Fri, 3pm-2am Sat & Sun; 🛜)

Crane's Bar DIVE BAR

25 Map p124, B3

From the graffed up concrete floor to the butcher-block bar (carved from a 130-year-old Douglas fir) to the red-vinyl booth to the underground bank-vault location (yes, this was a vault in another life), we love everything about DTLA's newest, sweetest and hottest dive. (☑323-787-7966; www.facebook.com/CranesDowntown; 810 S Spring St; ⏱5pm-late)

La Cita CLUB

26 Map p124, D3

The perfect setting for an afternoon that lasts until midnight or a wild soul-infused dance party, this red-vinyl Mexican dive bar alternates between a dance club and music venue for downtown hipsters, when DJs whip the crowd into a frenzy with hip-hop, soul, punk and whatever else gets people moving, and a live-band salsa party. (www.lacitabar.com; 336 S Hill St; ⏱10am-2am Mon-Fri, from 11am Sat & Sun)

Upstairs at the Ace Hotel BAR

27 Map p124, B3

Either lovingly cool, a bit too hip or a touch self-conscious depending upon your purview, there is no denying that downtown's newest rooftop bar – replete with magnificent views – opened to universal acclaim. (www.acehotel.com/losangeles; 929 S Broadway Ave; ⏱11am-2am)

Club Mayan CLUB

28 Map p124, A3

Kick up your heels during Saturday's Tropical Nights when a salsa band turns the heat up against the faux Mayan temple backdrop. Don't know how? Come early for lessons, but there is a dress code. On Fridays it's house and hip-hop, and the club also hosts its share of wrestling events, indie rockers like Jack White, and DJs with a following. (www.clubmayan.com; 1038 S Hill St; cover $10-25; ⏱9pm-3am Fri & Sat, varies Sun-Thu)

Entertainment

Nokia Theatre CONCERT VENUE

29 ⭐ Map p124, A1

A 7100-seat theater, christened by the Eagles and the Dixie Chicks when it

Staples Center

Staples Center (Map p124, A1; ☎213-742-7340; www.staplescenter.com; 1111 S Figueroa St; Ⓟ), aka the House that Shaq Built (and then bequeathed to one Kobe Bryant), is the vortex of pro basketball in LA. It is here that the **Los Angeles Lakers** (☎213-742-7340; www.nba.com/lakers; tickets $50-250) once reigned, and these days suffer in the shadow of Blake Griffin, Chris Paul and the Donald Sterling–stained **Los Angeles Clippers** (☎888-895-8662; www.nba.com/clippers; tickets $25-175).

opened in 2007, has since hosted Neil Young, Anita Baker and Bill Maher. Check the website for upcoming shows. (www.nokiatheatrelalive.com; 777 Chick Hearn Ct)

Music Center of LA County

PERFORMING ARTS

30 ⭐ Map p124, E2

At this linchpin of the downtown performing arts scene, splashy musicals play to capacity at the Ahmanson Theatre, while the more intimate Mark Taper Forum premieres high-caliber plays. With Placido Domingo at the helm, the LA Opera has fine-tuned its repertory of classics by master composers, with performances at the Dorothy Chandler pavilion. (☎213-972-7211; www.musiccenter.org; 135 N Grand Ave)

Orpheum Theatre

THEATER

31 ⭐ Map p124, B3

The 1920s Orpheum Theatre has been fully restored to host screenings and parties. Jam band gods Widespread Panic and younger phenoms MGMT played here recently. (☎877-677-4386; www.laorpheum.com; 842 S Broadway)

Shopping

Robert Reynolds Gallery

GALLERY

An incredible loft art space owned and operated by the artist himself. He specializes in mixed-media canvases and sculpture, and uses bamboo, Japanese paper and fiberglass to create fantasy boats and decaying lanterns, and crafts evocative landscapes from nails, straw, grass and wildflowers. Wow! Close to Bar Ama'. (see 11 Map p124, D3; ☎323-599-8485; www.robertreynolds.com; 408 S Spring St; ⊙11am-5pm Mon-Sat)

Jewelry District

JEWELRY

32 🔒 Map p124, C3

For bargain bling head to this bustling district, between 6th and 8th, where you can snap up watches, gold, silver and gemstones at up to 70% off retail. The mostly traditional designs are unlikely to be seen on the red carpet, but the selection is unquestionably huge. Quality varies. (www.lajd.net; Hill St)

Nokia Theatre (p133)

Hive
ART GALLERY

33 Map p124, C3

Nestled in a decidedly not-yet-gentrified stretch of Spring St is a seemingly small but surprisingly deep artist-owned gallery, where the art always delivers and the openings rock. (www.thehivegallery.com; 729 S Spring St; ☺1-6pm Wed-Sat)

Last Bookstore in Los Angeles
BOOKS

34 Map p124, D3

Who said the inky page is dead? What started as a one-man operation out of a Main St storefront is now nearly an entire ground floor of an old bank building, and it's stuffed with used books of all stripes as well as a terrific vinyl collection for musicologists. (www.lastbookstorela.com; 453 S Spring St; ☺10am-10pm Mon-Thu, to 11pm Fri & Sat, to 6pm Sun)

Top Sights
Exposition Park

Getting There

🚌 From downtown take I-110 S to I-10 W and exit at Vermont. Head south on Vermont and make a left on Exposition Blvd.

🚇 Metro Silver Line trains serve Exposition Park from their downtown hub.

A quick jaunt south of downtown via DASH bus, the family-friendly Exposition Park began as an agricultural fairground in 1872 and became the burgeoning city's public green space in 1913. The draws here are three high-quality museums and a robust, rambling rose garden. Not to mention the historic Los Angeles Memorial Coliseum, where the USC Trojans play (American) football.

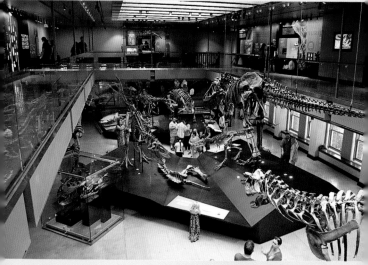

Natural History Museum

Don't Miss

Natural History Museum

Dinos to diamonds, bears to beetles, hissing roaches to African elephants – the Natural History Museum will take you around the world and back millions of years in time. It's all housed in a beautiful 1913 Renaissance-style building that stood in for Columbia University in the first Toby McGuire *Spider-Man* movie – yup, this was where Peter Parker was bitten by the radioactive arachnid.

California Science Center

The enormous California Science Center is divided into themed areas. Hitch a ride with a red blood cell for a computer fly-through of the human body. Explore human transportation and telecommunication systems as they evolve over time and visit desert, river, island, urban and forest habitats.

Astro Vintage

Technically part of the Science Center, aircraft and space travel take center stage in the adjacent **Sketch Foundation Gallery**.

Spaced Out

The Science Center is also home to Space Shuttle *Endeavour*. It's permanent home will be in a new gallery called the **Samuel Oschin Air and Space Center**, but while that's under construction you can see the beast in the **Samuel Oschin Pavilion**.

www.expositionpark. org

700 Exposition Park Dr

☑ Top Tips

▶ Admission to the museums is free on the first Tuesday of most months.

▶ Roam the Natural History Museum at night on First Fridays when the hipsters, and some families, invade for a lineup of live music and stellar DJs in the hallowed halls.

▶ When the butterfly and spider pavilions are up, it's best to buy your tickets in advance to ensure entry.

✕ Take a Break

Care for a blast of African American culture? Head to **Leimert Park** (Degnan Blvd & 43rd St), the community's cultural hub, where you can sample decadent barbecue, catch live jazz and comedy and peruse Pan-African handicrafts.

Local Life
Pasadena

Getting There

🚈 Metrolink's Gold Line serves Pasadena and connects it to downtown.

🚗 Take I-110 from downtown or the I-134 from Burbank.

One could argue that there is more blue-blood, meat-eating, robust Americana in Pasadena than in all other LA neighborhoods combined. Here is a community with a preppy old soul, a historical perspective, an appreciation for art and jazz and a slightly progressive undercurrent.

❶ Circumnavigate the Rose Bowl

One of LA's most venerable landmarks, the 1922 **Rose Bowl Stadium** (☎626-577-3100; www.rosebowlstadium. com; 1001 Rose Bowl Dr) can seat up to 93,000 spectators and has its moment in the sun every New Year's Day when it hosts the famous Rose Bowl postseason college football game. It is surrounded by **Brookside Park**, which is a nice spot for hiking, cycling and picnicking. Many locals run or pedal around the stadium each afternoon.

❷ Tour the Gamble House

It's the exquisite attention to detail that impresses most at the **Gamble House** (☎info 626-793-3334, tickets 800-979-3370; www.gamblehouse.org; 4 Westmoreland Pl; tours adult/child from $12.50/free; ☺tours noon-3pm Thu-Sun, gift shop 10am-5pm Tue-Sat, 11:30am-5pm Sun; **P**), a 1908 masterpiece of Craftsman architecture built by Charles and Henry Greene for Proctor & Gamble heir David Gamble.

❸ Enjoy World Class Art

Rodin's *The Thinker* is only a mind-teasing overture to the full symphony of art in store at this exquisite museum. The highly accessible, user-friendly galleries at **Norton Simon** (www.nortonsimon.org; 411 W Colorado Blvd; adult/child $10/free; ☺noon-6pm Wed-Mon, to 9pm Fri; **P**) teem with choice works by Rembrandt, Renoir, Raphael, Van Gogh, Botticelli and Picasso.

❹ A Steampunk Scene

An amazing boutique with a steampunk vibe, **Gold Bug** (☎626-744-9963; www.goldbugpasadena.com; 22 E Union St; ☺10am-5pm Mon, 10am-6pm Tue-Sat, noon-5pm Sun) shows work and collections created or curated by 100 area artists. We saw one robotic metallic Cheshire Cat, exquisite vintage jewelry and lamps, raw crystals and selenite and a terrific art book collection.

❺ California Style

The **Pasadena Museum of California Art** (www.pmcaonline.org; 490 E Union St; adult/student & senior/child $7/5/free, 1st Fri of month free; ☺noon-5pm Wed-Sun; **P**) is a progressive gallery dedicated to art, architecture and design created by California artists since 1850. Shows change every few months. The museum is free on the first Friday of every month.

❻ Dinner & Music

Dine on acclaimed Basque cuisine at the chef-owned **Racion** (☎626-396-3090; http://racionrestaurant.com; 119 W Green St; shared plates $5-27; ☺6-10pm Tue-Thu, 6-11pm Fri, 11am-2pm & 5:30-11pm Sat, 11am-2pm & 5:30-10pm Sun), then enjoy some of the best LA-area jazz talent doing their thing in **Red White & Bluezz'** (☎626-792-4441; www. redwhitebluezz.com; 37 S El Molino Ave; ☺10:30am-9pm Sun, from 11am Mon-Wed, 11am-11pm Thu, to midnight Fri & Sat) brassy Old Town environs. The latter also serves dinner.

Explore

Burbank & Universal City

Home to most of LA's major movie studios – including Warner Bros, Disney and Universal – the sprawling grid of suburbia known as 'the Valley' also has the dubious distinction of being the original world capital of porn, memorably captured in Paul Thomas Anderson's 1997 *Boogie Nights*.

The Sights in a Day

🔅 Breakfast at **Bob's Big Boy** (p149), Burbank's original drive-in diner, before heading over to **Warner Bros** (p146) for a working studio tour without the theme park attractions.

🔆 Grab lunch among the producers, aspiring writers and actors at **Daichan** (p146), then take the family to **Universal Studios** (p142) for an afternoon and evening of movie-loving adventure. The whole family will enjoy the **3-D Transformers ride** and the **Despicable Me Minion Mayhem**. If you've had your fill of the theme park disco, blitz over to **It's a Wrap!** (p149) before closing time.

🌙 If it's a balmy evening, stroll the **Universal CityWalk** (pictured left; p142). Otherwise, head over to Sushi Row for dinner at the undercover heaven that is **Asanebo** (p146) before letting the night fall around your shoulders at **Firefly** (p149).

 Top Sights

Universal Studios (p142)

💜 **Best of Los Angeles**

Eating
Asanebo (p146)

Getting There

Ⓜ **Metro** Universal City is well connected to Hollywood and downtown by the Metro Red Line, while Metrolink connects Burbank with downtown and Long Beach, and the Orange Line heads west into the San Fernando Valley.

Ⓜ **Metro** The most centrally located Red Line stop is Universal City.

Top Sights
Universal Studios

The magic of movie making gets its due at ever-popular Universal, one of the world's oldest continuously operating movie studios and theme parks, where thrill rides, live performances, interactive shows and back-lot tram tours perpetually draw the masses. Although it is a working studio, the chances of seeing any action, let alone a star, are slim.

⊙ Map p144, E5

www.universalstudios
hollywood.com

100 Universal City Plaza

admission from $87, under 3yr free

⊙open daily, hours vary

Don't Miss

Dive Into 3-D Mania

Shrek 4-D takes you from Lord Farquaad's dungeon into a theater where you'll don ogre-vision 3-D glasses and become immersed in the action. Nab a flight simulation thrill on the 3-D Transformers ride, or get lost in giggles on Dispicable Me Minion Mayhem.

Water World Show

The movie may have bombed, but the Water World show is a runaway hit. There are mind-boggling stunts such as giant fireballs and a crash-landing sea plane.

Universal CityWalk

With flashing video screens, oversized facades and garish color combinations, CityWalk hovers beside Universal Studios like a reject from the *Blade Runner*-meets-Willy Wonka school of architecture. Its 65 shops, restaurants and entertainment venues offer a mix of attractions, including the iFly vertical wind tunnel that mimics the feeling of skydiving.

☑ Top Tips

▶ Try to budget a full day, especially in summer. To beat the crowds, get here before the gates open or invest in the Front of Line Pass ($139) or the deluxe guided VIP Experience ($349).

▶ First-timers should head straight for the 45-minute narrated Studio Tour.

▶ The most popular thrill ride is Jurassic Park.

✕ Take a Break

There are plenty of dining choices at Universal CityWalk, but we suggest heading to Ventura Blvd's Sushi Row, where you can splurge or have sneaky-good affordable fare at **Daichan** (p146).

For reviews see

W Burbank Blvd

Clean Ave

North Hollywood

Ⓜ Chandler Blvd

North Hollywood Park

Weddington St

Vineland Ave

NORTH HOLLYWOOD

Dundas Dr

Magnolia Blvd

W Magnolia Blvd

Colfax Ave

Otsego St

2 ◎ Hartsook St

Bakman Ave

NoHo Arts District

Lankershim Blvd

Clean Ave

Riverside Dr

Camarillo St

Ventura Fwy

Tujunga Ave

Hollywood Fwy

Riverside Dr

Lankershim Blvd

Moorpark St

✘ 10

8 ✘ ✘ 9

Colfax Ave

4 7
✘ ✘

Arch Dr

◀️ 🅐 14 **Ventura Blvd**

12 🅟

Ventura Blvd ✘ 5

✘ 6

STUDIO CITY

Ⓝ 0 ———— 1 km
0 ———— 0.5 miles

Laurel Canyon Blvd

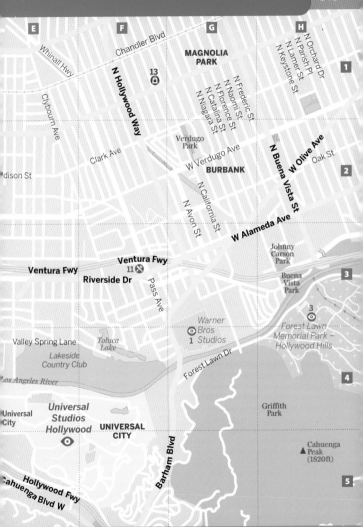

Sights

Warner Bros Studios
GUIDED TOUR

1 ⊙ Map p144, G4

This tour offers the most fun and an authentic look behind the scenes of a major movie studio. The 2½-hour romp kicks off with a video of WB's greatest film hits (*Rebel Without a Cause*, Harry Potter etc) before a tram whisks you to sound stages, back-lot sets and such departments as wardrobe and make-up. Reservations are required; bring photo ID. No children under 8 years. (☎818-972-8687, 877-492-8687; www.wbstudiotour.com; 3400 W Riverside Dr, Burbank; tours from $54; ⊙8:15am-4pm Mon-Sat, hours vary Sun)

NoHo Arts District
NEIGHBORHOOD

2 ⊙ Map p144, C2

Situated at the end of the Metro Red Line, North Hollywood (NoHo) was a down-on-its-heels neighborhood of artists, but thanks to a redevelopment it now boasts some 20 stage theaters in 1 sq mile and a burgeoning community of galleries, restaurants and vintage clothing stores that surround them. (www.nohoartsdistrict.com)

Forest Lawn Memorial Park – Hollywood Hills
CEMETERY

3 ⊙ Map p144, H3

Pathos, art and patriotism rule at this humongous cemetery next to Griffith Park. A fine catalog of old-time celebrities – including Lucille Ball, Bette Davis and Stan Laurel – rest within the manicured grounds strewn with paeans to early North American history. Download maps from the internet (eg www.seeing-stars.com), but be discreet or risk having them confiscated. (www.forestlawn.com; 6300 Forest Lawn Dr; admission free; ⊙8am-5pm; P)

Eating

Asanebo
SUSHI $$$

4 🍴 Map p144 , A4

Asanebo is a Michelin-star standout thanks to dishes such as halibut sashimi with fresh truffle, and *kanpachi* (yellowtail) with miso and serrano chilies. (☎818-760-3348; www.asanebo-restaurant.com; 11941 Ventura Blvd, Studio City; mains $3-21; ⊙noon-2pm & 6-10:30pm Tue-Fri, 6-10:30pm Sat, to 10pm Sun)

Kazu Sushi
JAPANESE $$$

5 🍴 Map p144, A4

Stuck in a cramped and otherwise nondescript split-level mini-mall that's easy to miss, Kazu is one of the best-kept secrets among LA's sushi aficionados. It's Michelin-rated, very high-end, has a terrific sake selection and is worth the splurge. (☎818-763-4836; 11440 Ventura Blvd, Studio City; dishes $10-19; ⊙noon-2pm & 6-10pm Mon-Sat; P)

Daichan
JAPANESE $$

6 🍴 Map p144, B4

Pasted with posters and staffed by the sunny and sweet owner-operator, this

Understand

The 'Industry'

From the moment film – and later TV – became the dominant entertainment medium, LA took center stage in the world of popular culture. It's also been the best (and sometimes the worst) ambassador of LA to the world. You might know it as entertainment, but to Angelenos it's simply the 'Industry.'

Entrepreneurial movie makers – most of them European immigrants – established studios here in the first decade of the 20th century. German-born Carl Laemmle built Universal Studios in 1915, selling lunch to curious guests coming to watch the magic of movie making; Polish immigrant Samuel Goldwyn joined with Cecil B DeMille to form Paramount Studios; and Jack Warner and his brothers arrived a few years later from Poland via Philadelphia. Perpetually sunny weather meant that most outdoor locations could be easily shot, and movie making flourished.

Fans loved early film stars such as Charlie Chaplin and Harold Lloyd, and the first big Hollywood wedding occurred in 1920 when Douglas Fairbanks wed Mary Pickford. What's more, the proximity of the Mexican border enabled filmmakers to rush their equipment to safety when challenged by the collection agents of patent holders such as Thomas Edison.

Although Hollywood became the cultural and financial hub of the movie industry, only Paramount Pictures is in Hollywood proper. Studios were built in Culver City (MGM, now Sony Pictures), Studio City (Universal Studios Hollywood) and Burbank (Disney and Warner Bros). The first big movie palaces were not on Hollywood Blvd but on Broadway in downtown LA.

Although LA sometimes feels like a company town, only about 150,000 people in LA County are employed in film, TV and radio production. That doesn't tell the whole story, though, because the Industry produces more jobs than that, from high-powered attorneys to cater-waiters. Still, there's more to LA than pretty moving pictures. Even if it doesn't always feel like it.

offbeat Japanese diner offers the best (and one of the tastiest) deals on Sushi Row. The fried seaweed tofu gyoza is divine and so are the bowls – especially the *negitoro* bowl, where fatty tuna is served over rice, lettuce and seaweed. (11288 Ventura Blvd, Studio City; mains $8.50-19; ⏰11:30am-3pm & 5:30-9pm Mon-Sat; Ⓟ)

La Ventura   MEXICAN $$

 7 Map p144, B4

There is one dish that makes Jeffrey Saad's latest upscale Mexican kitchen a destination all on its own. The lobster chorizo fundido incorporates crumbled layers of housemade chorizo and chunks of lobster, sautéed together then smothered in tequila cheese sauce and oven broiled. It's oily, it's spicy, it is culinary crack. (☎818-358-3423; www. laventurarestaurant.com; 11929 Ventura Blvd; mains $10-27; ⏰noon-11pm)

Suck It   FROZEN DESSERTS $

 8 Map p144, C3

Don't you dare call them popsicles! These are frozen desserts on a stick. The key-lime-pie flavor really is pie frozen on a stick. Same goes for coconut cream, Mexican hot chocolate and strawberry cheesecake. Everything is made in house by the owner and 'chief suckologist' (her words!). (☎818-980-7825; www.suckitsweets.com; 4361 1/2 Tujunga Ave, Studio City; desserts $4; ⏰1-8pm)

Caitoti Pizza Cafe   ITALIAN $$

 9 Map p144, C3

This long-time, long-loved Italian cafe does beet and spinach salads, bison burgers, Italian sausage sandwiches and some terrific pizzas and pastas. All served in an attractive concrete floor cafe where it can be tough to get a table at dinner time. (☎818-761-3588; www. caiotipizzacafe.com; 4346 Tujunga Ave, Studio City; mains $9-14; ⏰11am-10pm Mon-Thu, to 11pm Fri, 9am-11pm Sat, to 10pm Sun)

Aroma Coffee & Tea   CAFE $$

 10 Map p144, C3

A popular cafe where wood tables crowd heated patios on both sides and the line runs out the door thanks to goat cheese and walnut salads, popular turkey burgers, and breakfasts like chilaquiles (fried tortillas) and breakfast enchiladas, and a spinach puff pastry topped with scrambled eggs. (☎818-508-7377; www.aromacoffeeandtea. com; 4360 Tujunga Ave, Studio City; mains $9-14; ⏰6am-11pm Mon-Sat, from 7am Sun)

Bob's Big Boy   DINER $

11 Map p144, F3

Bob, that cheeky pompadoured kid in red checkered pants, hasn't aged a lick since serving his first double-decker in 1936. This Wayne McAllister–designed, Googie-style 1950s coffee shop is the oldest remaining Big Boy's in America. On Friday at about 4pm hot rods roar into the parking lot and stay all night, while the weekend car-hop service (5pm-10pm Saturday & Sunday) brings in families and lovers. (☑818-843-9334; www.bigboy.com; 4211 Riverside Dr, Burbank; burgers & sandwiches $7-10; ☺24hr; P 👬)

Drinking

Firefly   LOUNGE

12 Map p144, B4

Firefly has the sexiest library this side of an Anne Rice novel – bordello-red lighting, low-slung couches and flickering candles, surrounded by shelves of somber tomes. Not that anyone's opened one; the upwardly mobile crowd are too busy reading each other. (www.fireflystudiocity.com; 11720 Ventura Blvd, Studio City; ☺5pm-2am; 🚍MTA 150, 240)

Shopping

It's a Wrap!   VINTAGE

13 Map p144, F1

Here are fashionable, post-production wares worn by TV and film stars. What that means to you is great prices on mainstream designer labels, including racks of casual and formal gear worn on such shows as *Nurse Jackie*, *The Office* and *Scandal*. The suits are a steal, and so is the denim. New arrivals are racked by show affiliation. (www. itsawraphollywood.com; 3315 W Magnolia Blvd, Burbank; ☺10am-8pm Mon-Fri, 11am-6pm Sat & Sun)

Psychic Eye   NEW AGE

14 Map p144, A4

A longtime pipeline of psychics, astrologers, amulets, idols, books, candles and potions. If there's a spell you'd like to cast or break, if you need intuitive advice or would like to peer into the past or the future, find this strange vortex of the occult. (☑818-906-8263; www.pebooks. com; 13435 Ventura Blvd, Sherman Oaks; readings 15/30/60min $20/30/50; ☺10am-10pm Mon-Sat, to 8pm Sun)

✅ Top Tip

Be the Laugh Track

Half the fun of visiting LA is hoping you might see a star, so up the odds with a visit to the set of a prime-time sitcom. Multi-camera shows such as *Two and a Half Men* and *The Big Bang Theory* are shot before a live audience. That's you.

To nab tickets, check the website for **Audiences Unlimited** (www. tvtickets.com); to see what's taping, call ☑818-753-3470, or stop by the booth at Universal Studios (p142).

Top Sights
Disneyland & Disney California Adventure

Getting There

🚗 **Car** Anaheim is 25 miles southeast of downtown LA on I-5, exit Disneyland Dr.

🚆 **Train** Orange County line from Union Station to Anaheim Regional Transit Intermodal Center, then transfer.

Mickey is one lucky mouse. Created by animator Walt Disney in 1928, this irrepressible rodent is a multimedia juggernaut, and he lives in the 'Happiest Place on Earth.' The land of Disney is a slice of 'imagineered' hyper-reality, where the streets are always clean, the park employees – called cast members – are always upbeat, and there's a parade every day of the year. Even cynics must admit that since opening his home to guests in 1955, he's been a pretty thoughtful host to millions of blissed-out visitors.

Don't Miss

Main Street, USA

Fashioned after Walt's hometown of Marceline, Missouri, bustling Main St resembles the classic turn-of-the-20th-century, all-American town. It's an idyllic, relentlessly upbeat representation, complete with barbershop quartet, penny arcades, ice-cream shops and a steam train. **Great Moments with Mr. Lincoln**, a 15-minute audio-animatronics presentation, sits inside the fascinating Disneyland Story exhibit. Main St ends in the Central Plaza, lorded over by the iconic **Sleeping Beauty Castle**. On Main St there's a parade every evening.

Tomorrowland

Tomorrowland is a vision of what imagineers back in the 1950s thought the future might look like – monorails, rockets and Googie-like architecture. Today, most of the attractions have been updated, and the biggest thrills come from *Star Wars*–inspired **Star Tours**, with its Starspeeder 1000 rocketing through the big-screen desert canyons of Tatooine. **Space Mountain**, with its tight turns, screaming drops and blaring music, remains one of the park's most adrenaline-filled attractions. **Finding Nemo's Submarine Voyage** is an upcycled Disneyland classic, as are **Buzz Lightyear's Astro Blaster** and the tribute film **Captain EO**, starring Michael Jackson.

Fantasyland

Classic stories and characters dwell in Fantasyland, where the canal ride through **it's a small world** still charms. Hop aboard **Mr Toad's Wild Ride**, inspired by *The Wind in the Willows,* for a loopy jaunt through Mr Toad's mansion, underground London, Winky's Pub and, sadly, the courthouse. Younger kids love whirling around the **Mad Tea Party** teacup ride.

📞 714-781-4565

disneyland.disney.go.com

1313 Disneyland Dr

adult/child $96/90, both parks daypass adult/child $150/144

☑ Top Tips

▶ Disneyland Resort has three main areas: Disneyland Park and Disney California Adventure, both theme parks, and Downtown Disney, an outdoor pedestrian mall.

▶ To stay overnight (📞800-225-2024, reservations 714-956-6425; www.disneyland.com) try Disneyland Hotel or the stunning Disney's Grand Californian Hotel.

▶ Disneyland Resort is open every day. During peak summer season, Disneyland's hours are usually 8am to midnight; the rest of the year, 10am to 8pm or 10pm. DCA closes at 10pm or 11pm in summer, earlier in the off season.

✗ Take a Break

Mediocre fast-food and family restaurants are all over both parks.

Frontierland, New Orleans Square & Adventureland

The **Big Thunder Mountain Railroad** roller coaster awaits in Frontierland, where pioneers, miners and pirates live on. New Orleans Square houses the spooky but not too scary **Haunted Mansion** as well as the ever-popular 17-minute **Pirates of the Caribbean** boat ride. Yes, the ride was here first. **Indiana Jones** beckons from Adventureland with a lurching drive in an oversized jeep through an archaeologist's worst nightmare, or is it really his own twisted fantasy?

Do the Whammy

Have you gotten the Disneyland whammy yet? Don't worry, it's not a hex that cast members put on you for cutting in line. It's what fanatics call riding all three of Disneyland's 'mountain' rides – Splash Mountain (Critter Country), Space Mountain and the Big Thunder Mountain Railroad – in one day. Overachievers can jump on the Matterhorn Bobsleds (Fantasyland) for extra credit.

Disney California Adventure

Across the plaza from Disneyland's monument to make-believe is Disney California Adventure (DCA), an ode to California's geography, history and culture – or at least a sanitized G-rated version. DCA, which opened in 2001, covers more acres than Disneyland and feels less crowded, and it has more modern rides and attractions.

Understand

FASTPASS Attractions

Disneyland and DCA's FASTPASS system can significantly cut your wait times.

▶ Go to a FASTPASS ticket machine – near the entrance to select theme park rides – and insert your park entrance ticket or annual passport. You'll receive a slip of paper showing the 'return time' for boarding (it's always at least 40 minutes later).

▶ Show up within the window of time on the ticket and join the ride's FASTPASS line. There'll still be a wait, but it's shorter (typically 15 minutes or less). Hang on to your FASTPASS ticket until you board the ride.

▶ If you're running late and miss the time window printed on your FASTPASS ticket, you can still try joining the FASTPASS line, although showing up before your FASTPASS time window is a no-no.

▶ The catch? When you get a FAST-PASS, you will have to wait at least two hours before getting another one – so make it count.

The Twilight Zone Tower of Terror

The big attraction of **Hollywood Land**, if not the entire park, is The Twilight Zone Tower of Terror, a 13-story drop down an elevator chute situated in a haunted hotel – eerily

Monorail at Tomorrowland (p151), Disneyland

resembling the historic Hollywood Roosevelt Hotel in Los Angeles. From the upper floors of the tower, you'll have views of the Santa Ana Mountains, if only for a few heart-pounding seconds. The less brave can navigate a taxicab through 'Monstropolis' on the **Monsters, Inc: Mike & Sulley to the Rescue!** ride.

Golden State

Golden State is the adrenaline-addled sector of Disney California Adventure. Its main attraction, **Soarin' over California**, is a virtual hang glide using Omnimax technology that lets you float over landmarks such as the Golden Gate Bridge, Yosemite Falls, Lake Tahoe, Malibu and, of course, Disneyland itself. The **Grizzly River Run** takes you 'rafting' down a faux Sierra Nevada river – you will get wet, so come when it's warm. While fake flat-hatted park rangers look on, kids can tackle the **Redwood Creek Challenge Trail**, with its 'Big Sir' redwoods, wooden towers and lookouts, and rock slide and climbing traverses.

Paradise Pier

If you like carnival rides, you'll love Paradise Pier, designed to look like a combination of all the beachside amusement piers in California. The state-of-the-art **California Screamin'** roller coaster resembles

Understand
Fireworks, Parades, Oh My!

Remember – Dreams Come True, the fireworks spectacular above Sleeping Beauty Castle, happens nightly around 9:25pm in summer. In **Mickey's Soundsational Parade**, floats glide down Main Street USA with bands playing a variety of music from Latin to Bollywood, accompanying costumed characters.

At the **Princess Fantasy Faire** in Fantasyland, your little princesses and knights can join the Royal Court and meet some Disney princesses. Storytelling and coronation ceremonies happen throughout the day in summer. Younglings can learn to harness 'The Force' at **Jedi Training Academy**, which accepts Padawans several times daily in peak season, at Tomorrowland Terrace.

Fantasmic!, an outdoor extravaganza on Disneyland's Rivers of America, may be the best show of all, with its full-size ships, lasers and pyrotechnics, pink elephants, princesses and an evil queen. Arrive early to scope a spot – the best are down front by the water – or reserve balcony seats in New Orleans Square. Book reserved seating (☎714-781-7469, adult/child $60/50) up to 30 days in advance.

an old wooden coaster, but it's got a smooth-as-silk steel track: it feels like you're being shot out of a cannon. Just as popular is **Toy Story Midway Mania!**, a 4D ride where you earn points by shooting at targets while your carnival car swivels and careens through an oversize, old-fashioned game arcade.

Need for Speed
Based on the Disney·Pixar franchise, Cars Land is more than a ride, it's the newest section of DCA, complete with rides, shopping and dining options. You can glide through the air aboard **Luigi's Flying Tires**, and race through 6 acres of red-rock landscapes reaching speeds of up to 40mph at the **Radiator Springs Racers**.

Ariel's Undersea Adventure
Ariel's Undersea Adventure, patterned after Disneyland's Haunted Mansion ride, begins in a Victorian mansion where you'll hop aboard a clamshell that will transport you through underwater scenes of the classic film. All the stars – Ariel, Prince Eric, Sebastian and Flounder – will be waiting there to greet you.

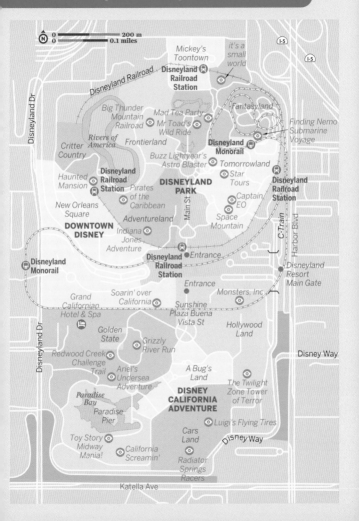

The Best of
Los Angeles

Los Angeles skyline at night
CHRIS HEPBURN/GETTY IMAGES ©

Best Walks
The Venice Stroll

🏃 The Walk

Step into the Venice lifestyle and rub shoulders with folks who believe that certain truths will only be revealed to those who disco-skate in a Speedo-and-turban ensemble. And, while such people may exist largely in their own universe, they happen to know that there are more moments of Zen packed into this tiny beach community than in most other 'hoods combined.

Start Ocean Front Walk and Washington Blvd; 🚌 BBB 1

Finish Abbot Kinney Blvd; 🚌 MTA 33

Length 3.5 miles; two hours

🍴 Take a Break

The best place to put your feet up is one of the many cafes and restaurants along Abbot Kinney Blvd. If you're hungry for a quick bite, consider **Abbot's Pizza** (p111), or tuck into something more substantial at **Joe's** (p110).

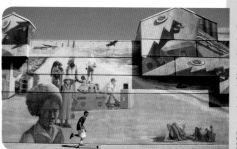

CHRIS CHEADLE/GETTY IMAGES ©

Venice Beach mural, *Endangered Species* by Emily Winters

❶ South Venice Beach

South of the Venice Pier is the untrammeled **beach** of South Venice.

❷ Venice Canals

Even many Angelenos have no idea that just a couple of blocks away from the boardwalk madness is an idyllic neighborhood that preserves 3 miles of **canals** of the late developer and tobacco mogul Abbot Kinney.

❸ Venice Boardwalk

The famed **Venice Boardwalk** (p106) is a vortex for the loony, the free-spirited, the hip and athletic. Here are outdoor gyms, beach rentals, skate parks and drum circles.

❹ Muscle Beach

Gym rats with an exhibitionist streak can get a tan and a workout at this famous **outdoor gym** (p107) right on the Venice Boardwalk where Arnold once bulked up alfresco.

MURAL COMMISSIONED BY SPARC (SOCIAL AND PUBLIC ART RESOURCE CENTER) THROUGH ITS GREAT WALLS UNLIMITED: NEIGHBORHOOD PRIDE PROGRAM,WITH SUPPORT FROM THE LOS ANGELES CULTURAL AFFAIRS DEPARTMENT (CR 1990 EMILY WINTERS, ARTIST)

6 Venice Beach Graffiti Park

Keep your camera at the ready as you approach the tagged-up towers and free standing concrete wall of **Venice Beach Graffiti Park** (p107), forever open to aerosol artists to curb vandalism.

6 Venice Beach Skate Park

Long the destination of local skate punks, the concrete at **Venice Beach Skate Park** (p107) has been molded and steel-fringed into 7,000 sq ft of vert, tranny and street terrain with unbroken ocean views.

7 Fig Tree's Café

If you're hungry already, **Fig Tree's Café** (p112) serves the best eats on the Boardwalk.

8 Ballerina Clown & the Chiat/Day Buildings

On Main St are two of Venice's more captivating buildings. The **ballerina clown** rises like a twisted god/goddess from the corner of Main and Rose on an otherwise pedestrian building. Across the street is Gehry's epic **Chiat/Day** building.

9 Abbot Kinney Boulevard

Abbot Kinney, the man who dug the canals and christened the town, would probably be delighted to find the stretch of his namesake **boulevard** (p109) stacked with unique, individually owned boutiques, galleries and sensational restaurants.

Best Walks
The Downtown Hustle

The Walk

Downtown is the most historical, multi-layered and fascinating part of Los Angeles. There's great architecture, from 19th-century beaux arts to futuristic Frank Gehry. There's world-class music at the Walt Disney Concert Hall, top-notch art at the Museum of Contemporary Art (MOCA), superb dining and a Fashion District. You'll see it all as you explore this power nexus, creative vortex and ethnic mosaic.

Start LA Live; **M**Pico

Finish Union Station; **M**Union Station

Length 3.8 miles; three hours

Take a Break

When you're doing the downtown hustle, the **Grand Central Market** (p126) is a good reason to pause. Both for its byzantine wholesale market and recently updated food stalls.

Union Station

❶ The Grammy Museum

Music lovers will get lost in interactive exhibits that define, differentiate and link musical genres, while live footage strobes from all corners at the **Grammy Museum** (p126). Easily the highlight of LA Live

❷ Fashion District

The axis of the **Fashion District**, this 90-block nirvana for shopaholics is the intersection of 9th and Los Angeles Sts where fashionistas and designers congregate.

❸ Broadway Theater District

Highlighted by the still-running **Orpheum Theatre** (p134), built in 1926, and the recently redone **United Artists Theatre** (p128), **Broadway** was LA's entertainment hub with no fewer than a dozen theaters built in a riot of styles.

❹ Pershing Square

The hub of downtown's historic core, **Pershing Square** was LA's first public park, and is now enlivened by public art and summer concerts.

❺ Grand Central Market

The ground floor of the 1905 Beaux-Arts **Grand Central Market** (p160) is where architect Frank Lloyd Wright once kept an office.

❻ Museum of Contemporary Art

The **Museum of Contemporary Art** (p126), housed in a building by Arata Isozaki, has a collection that arcs from the 1940s and includes works by Mark Rothko and Dan Flavin.

❼ Walt Disney Concert Hall

A molten blend of steel, music and psychedelic architecture, Gehry pulled out all the stops for the iconic **Walt Disney Concert Hall** (p120).

❽ Pueblo de Los Angeles

Here's where LA's first colonists settled in 1781. **Pueblo de Los Angeles** (p126) preserves the city's oldest buildings.

❾ Union Station

A glamorous Mission Revival achievement with art deco accents, **Union Station** (p126) opened in 1939 as America's last grand rail station. Bukowski worked at the historic Terminal Annex post office just north of the station.

Best
Food

As recently as a decade ago, Los Angeles was often overlooked when it came to the world's best eating cities. Yet it was here that celebrity chefs such as Nobu Matsuhisa and Wolfgang Puck rose to stardom, where market-fresh health food first morphed into cuisine, and where the diversity of culture and community have converged into some of the best ethnic kitchens in America.

The Big Shots

OK, so somewhere along the way chefs became celebrities, and the kitchen became a stage, and that arguably all started in Beverly Hills with Wolfgang Puck and Spago in the 1980s. It's also true that ever since then the world's best chefs have flocked to these celebrified streets to serve power lunches and dinners, and bask in the glow of Hollywood stars, and then partner with them. These days, chefs such as the aforementioned Matsuhisa, Thomas Keller, Mario Batali, Brooke Williamson and Michael Voltaggio are among the culinary celebs ready to serve you.

Ethnic Pride

The pride we speak of is not simply the kind inherent in any proud, culturally awake and aware chef poised to share his or her tradition with their ravenous public. It's the kind of pride that Angelenos often feel when they've tasted flavors that explode in new directions, when the food they eat tells some other kind of story that gets their mind bounding around the world. And it's the pride in sharing their discovery over a long, wine-drenched meal with family and friends.

☑ Top Tips

▶ Check Pulitzer Prize winner Jonathan Gold's column in the *LA Times* for more off the beaten ethnic kitchens and gourmet prose.

▶ LA restaurants fill up between 7pm and 9pm, but if you don't mind dining late, arrive after 9pm and you won't wait long for a table.

Best Deli & Market Cafes

Forage Think bread pudding to pear-and-frangipani galettes, and pork belly sandwiches, too. (p48)

Huckleberry Crowds keep coming for the

turkey-meatball sandwich and deli salads. (p96)

Tasting Kitchen A terrific destination restaurant serving equally marvelous cocktails. (p110)

Ray's Where culinary art meets fine art at the LACMA. (p81)

Milo & Olive Baked eggs at breakfast and pizzas and small plates at dinner. (p95)

Best Celeb Kitchens

Pizzeria Mozza Thin-crust pies come with squash blossoms and mozzarella among other delights. (p30)

Bestia LA's hot new table serves up artful, Italian-inspired cuisine. (p130)

Bar Ama' Everything from pig ears to enchiladas with mole sauce. (p128)

Bar Pintxo Tapas, paella, great wine and a shot of Spanish soul. (p95)

Best Ethnic Eateries

Sushi Gen Thick slabs of melt-in-your-mouth salmon, buttery toro and a wonderful Japanese snapper. (p131)

Jitlada A transporting taste of southern Thailand. (p31)

Woodspoon Pork ribs that fall off the bone, fried yucca and pot pies. (p129)

Asanebo Michelin-starred sushi with truffles and serrano chiles. (p146)

Best Seafood

Son of a Gun Less classic, more edge at this tasty seafood haunt. (p79)

Connie & Ted's A throwback, festive East Coast seafood house. (p59)

Best Veggie Vortex

Elf Cafe Start with feta wrapped in grape leaves then move on to a fantastic kebab of seared oyster mushrooms. (p47)

Sage & Kind Kreme An organic vegan cafe serving fantastic raw, vegan ice cream. (p53)

Real Food Daily Ann Gentry's famous kitchen still satisfies even devout carnivores. (p97)

Best
Drinking

Dry and dusty LA may be, but you will not go thirsty. After all, this is the town of Lebowski and Bukowski, and where Kiefer Sutherland and Gary Oldman's legendary long lunch led to Oldman's DWI arrest in the wee small hours. LA is where Slash discovered Jack Daniels, and where some of America's most creative bartenders mix and muddle craft cocktails with a smirk or a smile.

The Brothers Houston

The Houston Brothers, 35-year-old fraternal twins, practically grew up behind a bar. Their mother owned her share of restaurants and watering holes, so they had the hospitality business in their blood. Still, when they bought the Piano Bar in Hollywood, nobody could have predicted their rise to the top of LA's nightlife scene. But thanks to a melding of set piece design, live burlesque dancers and top-shelf cocktails and spirits – first unveiled at La Descarga and replicated at Harvard & Stone and No Vacancy – that's exactly where they've landed. Their latest is Good Times At Davey Wayne's, a perfect place to start the night.

Simple & Straight

Some of us prefer not to have complexities such as pomegranate or grapefruit juice; simple syrup and freshly snipped herbs get in the way of a fine spirit. Does this mean we lack taste? It simply suggests that when we go out drinking, we seek establishments that serve only the best rums, tequilas, mescals, whiskeys and bourbons distilled from this sweet earth, and when we finally arrive at the bar, we peruse the selection, order something generally high end, usually aged, and always neat.

☑ Top Tips

▶ To minimize mortal injury to yourself and others, get to know an LA niche by strategically sampling bars within walking distance of one another. Cab or Uber it back to the hotel and do it all over again tomorrow.

▶ Downtown offers countless hip and tasty scenes within a short stroll.

Best Muddlers

Copa d'Oro Addictive cocktails crafted from a well of top-end spirits and a produce bin of fresh herbs, fruits, juices and a few veggies too. (p98)

Venice Beach Wines (p113)

Comme Ca The brainy barmen serve prohibition-era cocktails – meaning they only use what was available during the 1920s and 1930s. (p62)

No Vacancy Tight-rope walkers, creative cocktails, burlesque dancers and lots of pretty people. (p33)

Basement Tavern Quasi speakeasy beneath a historic Victorian in Santa Monica with live music. (p98)

Varnish A backroom downtown speakeasy with live music. (p131)

Best Hard Stuff

El Carmen LA's ultimate tequila and mescal tavern with over 100 to choose from. (p81)

Las Perlas Old Mexico whimsy and a chalkboard menu of over 80 tequilas and mescals. (p132)

Harvard & Stone Craft whiskey, bourbon and daily cocktail specials. (p35)

Bar Marmont A Sunset Strip classic that still delivers midweek. (p62)

Best Wine & Beer Bar

Venice Beach Wines Intimate indoor-outdoor neighborhood wine bar. (p113)

Best Dives

Short Stop Laid back, funky and sprawling with a sweaty dance floor. (p49)

Thirsty Crow Where bourbon is the preferred poison. (p49)

Best
Live Music

Live music should be considered a natural resource. Like nature, its presence affects moods and circumstance; it can also inspire new creativity, technology and economies. It's a nourishing flow that fertilizes the seeds of catharsis, loosens the intellect and enlivens the spirit. So go get some!

WIREIMAGE/GETTY IMAGES ©

Night Music

Just like the perfect set of waves, or that first spring rain you can never be quite sure when, or if, it will happen. You do know that if your fellows are open of mind, and the musicians of the moment are generous of heart, that there will be the possibility of greatness; of feeling new and alive in the Southern California night.

Whether they be the hippie rockers and electronic mixologists of Echo Park, or the jazz cats of LACMA, whether they belong to the local philharmonic or are simply blasting through town and exploding on legendary stages like the global pop virtuosos they have become, there will be night music in Angel City. Download the Bandsintown smart phone app for daily listings.

Best Stages

Hollywood Bowl LA's greatest gift to musicians and their fans. (p28)

Greek Theatre Almost as perfect as the Bowl. (p50)

El Rey A converted movie theater which hosts terrific indie acts. (p82)

Echo & Echoplex An edgy mix of DJ-driven dance parties and new rockers. (p53)

Fonda Theatre Hosts rising acts and residencies from legends like Tom Petty. (p35)

Best Free Concert Venues

LACMA Friday means live jazz on the plaza for six months a year. (p74)

California Plaza World music delights a packed plaza during the summer. (p127)

Getty Center Off the 405 events bring in alt rockers and world music. (p69)

Santa Monica Pier Thursday nights bring live music throughout the summer. (p90)

Bardot Their Monday 'It's A School Night' club is a curated showcase for up and comers. (p36)

Best
Gay & Lesbian

RICHARD CUMMINS/GETTY IMAGES ©

LA is one of the country's gayest cities. Your gaydar may well be pinging throughout the county, but the rainbow flag flies especially proudly in Boystown, along Santa Monica Blvd in West Hollywood (WeHo), flanked by dozens of high-energy bars, cafes, restaurants, gyms and clubs. Most cater to gay men, but there's plenty for lesbians and mixed audiences. Thursday to Sunday nights are prime.

Scoping the Scene

Beauty reigns supreme among the buff, bronzed and styled of Boystown. Elsewhere, the scene is more laid-back and less body-conscious. The crowd in Silver Lake runs from cute hipsters to leather-and-Levi's bears and an older contingent. Venice and Long Beach have the most relaxed, neighborly scenes.

Except for the hardcore places, LA's gay spots get their share of opposite-sex and straight patrons, drawn by gay friends, the fabulousness of the venues and abundant eye candy.

The Arts

There's gay theater all over town, but the Celebration Theatre ranks among the nation's leading stages for LGBT plays. West Hollywood's annual Halloween Carnival draws a crowd of 500,000 to Santa Monica Blvd. June's LA Gay Pride parade and festival (www.lapride. org) is a celebration of diversity that brings huge crowds to the neighborhood with exhibits and shows.

The annual AIDS walk attracts thousands of fundraisers to the starting line at the Pacific Design Center.

Best Nightspots

Abbey (p63) Match your mood to the many different spaces, from outdoor patio to Goth lounge to chill room.

Eleven (www.eleven.la; 8811 Santa Monica Blvd; ⏱5pm-2am Mon-Thu, to 3am Fri, noon-3am Sat, 11am-2am Sun) A glam spot in a historic building hosting high energy dance parties.

Micky's (www.mickys. com; 8857 Santa Monica Blvd; ⏱5pm-2am Sun-Thu, to 4am Fri & Sat) Quintessential WeHo dance club, with go-go boys, expensive drinks and plenty of eye candy.

Best
Shopping

CHRISTIAN THOMAS/GETTY IMAGES ©

There's no other way to really say it. Angelenos are compulsive shoppers. You can buy anything here. A human skull? Check. A three-speed vibrator with multiple attachments? Check. A vintage, turn-of-the-century Parisian baby doll dress? Check. Japanimation action figures for grown-up hipsters? Yes! Not to mention some of the best and worst fashion ever to come out of any workshop.

High End, Darling

Heavyweight fashion houses cluster around Melrose Pl, and Fred Segal has two such outposts. Just know that if you do enter these hallowed halls, you will want to buy everything, compulsively seek out ever more obscene price tags in a blind 'but-I-want-these!' rage and you may whimper, even as you fork over a week's pay for a pair of stockings or some eyeliner. But, hey, this is LA, baby. There's no crying at the register!

Keep it Indie, Keep it Local

Here's the one knock on the indie shops, labels and boutiques: they're all so damn expensive when compared to the Banana Republics of the world. But if you're into shopping with honor, and espouse a 'do no harm' lifestyle, then you will seek out LA's indie boutiques. You might make a sample sale in the Fashion District, and hunt down start-up designers on the Silver Lake streets.

House of Quirk (& Smut)

If you are partial to midnight screenings of the *Rocky Horror Picture Show,* and enjoy the strange microtastes of all-over-the-map gift shops and genre bending sex-shops, then LA is your Neverland.

☑ Top Tips

▶ Save gas and aggravation by conquering LA-area boutiques a neighborhood at a time.

▶ LA's farmers markets are not just great places to brunch and people-watch – young indie designers often set up stalls offering boho wear and elegant jewelry.

Best of the Best

Barneys New York LA's best department store. They have a warehouse sale twice a year. (p67)

Reformation Accessible fashion with an ecological ethos. (p65)

Browsing a vintage shop

Diane von Furstenberg
You know the lady. She
deals in high-end couture.
(p66)

Fred Segal A decon-
structed department
store with choice fashion
offerings. Celebs love it.
(p65)

Lotta Boutique A breezy
boutique stocked with
divine dresses that have
lured in Beyoncé on the
regular. (p84)

Abbot Kinney Blvd
Unique boutiques,
galleries, lofts and
vintage clothing stores.
(p109)

Best Offbeat

Spitfire Girl Our favorite
gift shop in the city is
a quirky cute staple.
(p51)

OK A brainy gift shop
geared toward those with
refined taste and dispos-
able income. (p85)

Wacko A warehouse of
kitsch, with a welcome
literary impulse. (p51)

Best Rummage

**Fashion District Sample
Sales** Dig for hidden
gems among the indie
design workshops. (p123)

Melrose Trading Post
A dreamy flea market
at Fairfax High School.
(p67)

Espionage Tasteful melange of new and vintage
goods. (p84)

Best
For Kids

Looking around Dr, Sunset Strip and down-town's Fashion District, it's easy to think that LA's children have been banished to a gingerbread cottage in the woods. But the kids are here. And they have loads of stuff to do.

GARY VESTAL/GETTY IMAGES ©

Get to Know the Nodes

The term in city planning these days is 'nodes' (art nodes, shopping nodes) – islands of specificity dotting the urban landscape. Kid-friendly nodes include the beaches, where parents can wear out their tykes with cycling and swimming, as well as LA's parks, where hiking, exploring and animal-watching are top notch.

Young *Animal Planet* devotees can ogle hu-manesque chimps at Griffith Park's LA Zoo, while future paleontologists can study skeletal sabre-toothed cats pulled from the La Brea Tar Pits. And, of course, don't forget the kiddiest nodes of all, theme parks, with options ranging from all-day happiness at Disneyland and Universal Studios to momentary thrills at Pacific Park.

Long Beach is another wonderful node, as here you'll find the exceptional Aquarium of the Pacific, which can take a full day, as well as the Queen Mary, where you can enjoy the hokey but fun Ghost & Legends Tour, and the stunning Point Fermin Park in nearby San Pedro.

Best Animal-Watching

Los Angeles Zoo 1100 finned, feathered and furry friends from over 250 species. (p46)

Best Outdoor Fun

Griffith Park One of the country's largest urban green spaces and one perfect carousel. (p47)

Echo Park Lake Take a pedal boat or a canoe out among the ducks, swans and the gushing fountain. (p53)

Manhattan Beach A gor-geous sweep of golden sand walking distance from an ice-cream parlor that might change your life. (p116)

Santa Monica Pier & Beach Kids love the venerable pier, where attractions include a quaint carousel, a solar-powered Ferris wheel and tiny aquarium with touch tanks. The beach ain't bad either. (p90)

Best Kid-Friendly Museums

Griffith Observatory Grab a seat in the planetarium by day, peer into telescopes on the lawn by night. (p42)

California Science Center A simulated earthquake, baby chicks

hatching and a giant techno-doll named Tess bring out the kid in all of us. The spacecraft rock too! (p137)

Natural History Museum This museum will take you around the world and back millions of years in time. (p137)

Best Kid-Friendly Restaurants

Uncle Bill's Pancake House Grab an ocean-view table among the sexy surfers, tottering toddlers and gabbing girlfriends – everybody's

here for the famous pancakes! (p117)

Abbot's Pizza Co Kids dig pizza. Yes, they do. (p158)

Original Farmers Market A jumble of stalls and restaurants. Even the most finicky eaters can find something agreeable here. (p81)

◆ Worth a Trip

Long Beach's most mesmerizing experience, the **Aquarium of the Pacific** (☏tickets 562-590-3100; www.aquariumofpacific.org; 100 Aquarium Way, Long Beach; adult/senior/child $29/26/15; ◷9am-6pm; ♿) is a vast, high-tech indoor ocean where sharks dart, jellyfish dance and sea lions frolic. Over 12,000 creatures inhabit four re-created habitats: the bays of Baja, the northern Pacific, tropical coral reefs and local kelp forests.

Best
Outdoor
Adventure

With bike paths, mountain trails, pounding surf and wind-blown seas only minutes away, the question isn't whether you should enjoy the outdoors, but how?

DAYNNA SHANNON/GETTY IMAGES ©

Get Physical

Hollywood visitors short on time can zip a loop around Runyon Canyon northwest of La Brea Ave, where a steep uphill climb, great views and a no-leash policy lures Hollywood hipsters and their pooches. Griffith Park boasts 53 miles of trails plus the iconic hike to the summit of Mt Hollywood (*not* the location of the sign), where stellar 360-degree views await, smog-willing. Tree-lined trails along the coastal mountains offer ocean and canyon views, while cyclists bounce along the Backbone Trail down the southern spine of the Santa Monicas. Beach cruisers may prefer the flat 22-mile South Bay Bicycle Trail from Santa Monica to within a spoke of Palos Verdes.

Don't like exercising alone? John Muir's 110-year-old Sierra Club lets nonmembers join its organized, very welcoming hikes and bike rides, geared to various fitness levels. See www. angeles.sierraclub.org to choose from hundreds of options. The night hikes are especially cool. Mountain-bikers should check www. corbamtb.com and www.socalmtb.com for conditions.

Best Short Hikes with Views

Hollyridge Trail Part of Griffith Park but best accessed from Bronson Canyon, this trail leads to just below the Hollywood Sign (p42)

Runyon Canyon It's a hike, it's a workout, it's a pick-up spot with a view. (p58)

Best Ease-of-Access Cycling

South Bay Bicycle Trail Pedal from Santa Monica to Redondo Beach. (p90)

Griffith Park You can rent a bike here then ride the trails. (p47)

Best
Beaches

The stars of *Baywatch*, *The OC* and *Laguna Beach* weren't the first photogenic faces to inspire waves of California dreamin'. Nope, that would be George Freeth – one part Irish, one part Hawaiian and one part Victorian surf god – who arrived on LA's shores 100 years ago with a wooden surfboard to promote Hawaiian tourism. But tycoon and local booster Henry Huntington persuaded young George to stick around, paying him to surf in front of his hotel. Tourists and locals were hooked, and California surf culture was born.

MARCUS LINDSTROM/GETTY IMAGES ©

Beach Life at its Best

Today, surfers head to Malibu's Surfrider beach, while South Bay wave hounds check out Manhattan Beach. But it's not all about the perfect break. Santa Monica's wide sandy swath is perfect for quintessential beach living – volleyball, body-surfing and sunbathing are top-notch. Same goes for Manhattan and the beach south of the Venice Pier, where the crowds are lighter.

For rambling, El Matador and Westward Beach near Point Dume offer big nature. That's where the seals, sea lions and dolphins play and breach for lucky beachcombers. If you encounter beachside fencing, unleash your inner libertarian and defy them! According to California law, all beaches are public.

Best People-Watching

Venice Boardwalk
Let your freak flag fly! (p106)

Manhattan Beach
Ample sand space, tasty waves. (p116)

Santa Monica Beach
The best choice for families. (p90)

Best for Beachcombing

El Matador Rocky spires in the swirling tides. (p103)

Westward Beach A wide beach, clear waters, dolphins, sea lions and migrating whales. (p103)

Surfrider If you dare not paddle out, you can at least watch the surfers do their thing as your stroll the sand. (p103)

Best Celebrity-Spotting

Admit it. You want to see a celeb. Of course you do. You're in Hollywood. So don't apologize for it. Prophets, poets, professional actors – people are drawn to a famous face. Maybe it's the talent we love, or feeling connected to the world through one anointed person, or thinking we'll absorb a bit of the holy glow. Or maybe they're just hot and cool, or...hot.

Getting Your Star Fix

The University of Southern California published a study finding that actors tend to be more narcissistic than the rest of society. Uh, yeah, and too much cheese is fattening. That said, it suggests that fan-love sates their needs as well as your own.

So, how to fulfill two needs with one gawk? Driving past stars' homes is a start, but it's unlikely you'll see anyone. As for velvet-rope clubs, you very well may not get in. So where to look for stars? In their natural habitat, of course. Restaurants are primo, especially in Hollywood, West Hollywood and Mid-City. As for cinemas, spotting celebs at the ArcLight is a good bet. Shopping works too, so browse their faves on Robertson Blvd and Abbot Kinney Blvd. Finally, hillside trails are favored for exercise. Who was that jogging past in the baseball cap?

Best Celebrity-Spotting Restaurants

Dan Tana's High-end dining and late-night supper lures big stars. (p60)

AOC A long-running celebrity-spotting glitterati favorite. (p80)

Ita Cho A staple for celebs in the West Hollywood swirl. (p79)

Popular Celeb-Spotting Spots

Fred Segal Top-shelf shopping yields top-shelf shoppers. (p65)

Barneys New York Celebs often peruse the stock and dine at the top-floor deli. (p67)

Malibu Country Mart Many stars live in 'the Bu,' and this is the only shopping and dining vortex in town. (p103)

Celeb Sighting Almost Guaranteed

Runyon Canyon Weekdays only. (p58)

Bar Marmont Weeknights only. (p62)

Warner Bros Studio VIP Tour They work here, don't they? (p176)

Best
Museums

Museums grand and austere, sprawling and magical, tucked away and hidden in plain sight, dot the Greater Los Angeles Area. Among them are Shinto shrines, a window into 'Jurassic technology,' a part-time jazz hub, prehistoric remains, and a museum masterwork that is stuffed with so many of Getty's goodies it's almost unfathomable. If you're not feeling culturally aware, awake or relevant in LA, you won't be alone, but it will be your own fault.

MOCA MUSEUM OF CONTEMPORARY ART 'TRAVEL INK/GETTY IMAGES ©

Best Museums

Getty Center Stunning location, groundbreaking architecture, rotating exhibits and timeless treasures. (p69)

LACMA LA's top art museum, stocked with fine art and global antiquities. (p74)

MOCA Works by Mark Rothko, Dan Flavin and Joseph Cornell housed in a postmodern building by Arata Isozaki. (p126)

Hammer Museum Minor works by Monet, Van Gogh and Mary Cassat, and cutting-edge contemporary exhibits. (p58)

Best Alternative Realities

Museum of Jurassic Technology Be warned, there is madness lurking in this rabbit hole. (p87)

Jadis A steampunk gallery of old film props and analog robots. (p94)

Grammy Museum If you're a music nerd, come here and trace the history of American popular music. (p126)

Wall Project A fat slab of the fallen Berlin Wall blessed with work from street artists, via the Wende Museum. (p78)

☑ Top Tips

▶ Most, if not all, of LA-area museums offer specific 'free days' to their public. Some are free all day once a week, or once or twice monthly, and still others offer a few hours free a week.

▶ The Anne Frank Exhibit at the Museum of Tolerance is sensational.

Best
Tours

Whether you're interested in the seeds of LA noir, ghost hunting, ethnic nibbling, soaking in neon, architecture, art, or peering at the many sides of the angel city from a road bike, beach cruiser or double-decker bus, we've got you covered.

Get Deep, Get Weird, Get Real

Whatever your pleasure – dark or light, tragic or profane, sweet and tasty – there is a tour for you. There exists a tour of scandal and blood, you may gawk at the stars (and their dirt) with actual paparazzi, tour a working studio in Burbank, gaze at world-class architecture downtown, and buzz between blasts of aerosol artistry on the Metro.

Best Tours

Dearly Departed Tours (☎855-600-3323; www. dearlydepartedtours.com; 6603 Sunset Blvd; tours $48) Explore the Manson murders, Janis' overdose,

Whitney's decline and Michael's greatness and dysfunctional sadness.

TMZ Tours (☎855-4TMZ-TOUR; www.tmz.com/tour; 6925 Hollywood Blvd; adult/child $55/45; ⊙approx 10 tours daily) Join this branded tour imagined by the paparazzi made famous. Tours are two hours long, and you will likely meet TMZ stars and perhaps even celebrity guests on the bus!

Warner Bros Studio VIP Tour (☎818-972-8687, 877-492-8687; www. wbstudiotour.com; 3400 W Riverside Dr, Burbank; tours from $54; ⊙8:15am-4pm Mon-Sat, hours vary Sun) See the inner workings of a real movie studio.

Esotouric (☎323-223-2767; www.esotouric.com;

tours $58) The great capers, the notorious crimes and the best writers are all tour fodder.

Metro Rail Art (www. metro.net/about/art/art-tours; ⊙10am 1st Sat & Sun of month) Some of LA's best contemporary art is not in a museum but in its Metro stations. Discover works by Jonathan Borowsky and Gilbert 'Magu' Lujan, among others.

Los Angeles Conservancy (☎213-430-4219 info, ☎213-623-2489 reservations; www.laconservancy. org; adult/child $10/5) Downtown LA's intriguing historical and architectural gems are revealed on 2½-hour walking tours.

Survival Guide

Survival Guide

Before You Go

When to Go

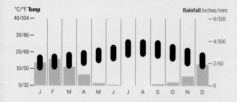

°C/°F Temp
40/104 —
30/86 —
20/68 —
10/50 —
0/32 —

J F M A M J J A S O N D

Rainfall Inches/mm
— 6/150
— 4/100
— 2/50
— 0

➡ **Spring (Apr-Jun)** Wild-flowers bloom in the hills, rain is scarce and the sun shines warm on southern California.

➡ **Summer (Jul-Sep)** Inland temperatures begin to soar and air quality suffers. By the sea, overcast skies (aka June Gloom) can persist through July.

➡ **Autumn (Oct-Dec)** The first of LA's two short wet seasons begins in October. Between storms temperatures stay in the 70s and the skies are blue.

➡ **Winter (Jan-Mar)** The more significant rainy season; it's also when mountains appear snow-glazed beyond downtown and wildflowers bloom.

Book Your Stay

When choosing overnight digs in Los Angeles, pick your location wisely. Staying at a beach hotel is probably not the best choice if you're catching a performance at Walt Disney Concert Hall or visiting Universal Studios in Burbank. Most neighborhoods have hotels in just about every price range. Expect to pay between $130 and $200 per night for a midrange room.

Useful Websites

Los Angeles Hotel Accommodations (www.losangeleshotelaccommodations.com) A local discount online booking site.

Orbitz (www.orbitz.com) It offers discounted rates, but always cross-check with the hotel's own website to be sure.

Lonely Planet (www.lonelyplanet.com) Author-penned reviews and online booking.

Best Budget

ibe Hotel (www.vibehotel.
m) A funky motel
rned hostel with both
-ed and female-only
orms – each with a flat
creen and kitchenette,
nd several recently
-done private rooms
at sleep three. You'll
are space with a
appening international
owd.

SA Hostels Hollywood
ww.usahostels.com) This
ociable hostel puts
u within steps of the
ollywood party circuit.
rivate rooms are a bit
amped, but making
ew friends is easy during
aff-organized barbe-
es, comedy nights and
25 all-you-can-drink
no tours.

Best Midrange

ali Hotel (www.pali-hotel.
m) We love the rustic
ood-panelled exterior,
e polished-concrete
oor in the lobby, the Thai
assage spa (just $35
r 30 minutes), and the
2 contemporary rooms
ith two-tone paint jobs,
all-mounted flat-screen,
nd enough room for a
ofa. Some have terraces.

**Venice Beach Inn &
Suites** (www.venicebeach
suites.com) This good-
value place right on the
Boardwalk scores big for
its bend-over-backwards
staff, and bevy of beach
toys for rent. There are
exposed-brick walls,
kitchenettes, wood floors
and built-in closets.

Best Top End

Petit Ermitage (www.
petitermitage.com) If you're
drawn to bohemian-chic
environs with Turkish
rugs, old-world antiques,
rooftop bars and fine
booze, then these suites
may be for you. This
intimate boutique hotel
offers suites with a wet
bar and kitchenette,
featuring Venetian-style
plaster walls. And the
rooftop pool, surrounded
by the Hollywood Hills,
will make you smile.

Ace Hotel (www.acehotel.
com/losangeles) Either
lovingly cool, a bit too hip
or a touch self-conscious
depending upon your
purview, there is no
denying that downtown's
newest hotel opened
to universal acclaim.
And the minds behind it
care deeply about their

product. Some rooms are
cubby-box small, but the
'medium' rooms work.

Arriving in Los Angeles

☑ **Top Tip** For the best
way to get to your accom-
modations, see p17.

Los Angeles International Airport

**Los Angeles Interna-
tional Airport** (LAX;
☎ 310-646-5252; www.lawa.
org/lax; 1 World Way; 🛜) is
about 17 miles southwest
of downtown, bounded by
the Pacific Ocean to the
west and the San Diego
Fwy (I-405) to the east.

➡ All nine terminals are
linked by the free Shuttle
A leaving from the lower
(arrival) level. Cabs and
hotel and car-rental shut-
tles stop here as well.

➡ Curbside dispatch-
ers will summon a taxi
for you. The flat rate to
downtown LA is $47,
while going to Santa Mon-
ica costs $30 to $35, to

West Hollywood around $40, to Hollywood to $50 and to Disneyland $90.

➡ Public transportation has become a lot easier since the arrival of **LAX FlyAway** (☎866-435-9529; www.lawa.org; one way $8). These buses travel nonstop to downtown's Union Station ($8, 45 minutes), Van Nuys ($8, 45 minutes), Westwood Village near UCLA ($10, 30 minutes), and to the Expo Line Light Rail station at La Brea and Exposition Blvd ($7; 1¼ hours) for connections to South Central, Hollywood and Union Station.

➡ For Santa Monica or Venice, catch the free Shuttle C bus to the **LAX City Bus Center & MetroRail Station** (96th St & Sepulveda Blvd), then change to the Santa Monica Rapid 3 ($1, one hour). The center is the hub for buses serving all of LA. If you're headed

for Culver City, catch Culver City bus 6 ($1, 20 minutes). For Manhattan or Hermosa Beach, hop aboard Beach Cities Transit 109 ($1), which also stops at Lot G. For Redondo Beach head to Lot C and hop the Metro Local 232 ($1.75). Trip-planning help is available at www.metro.net.

➡ The Disneyland Resort Express travels hourly or half-hourly from LAX to the main Disneyland resorts (adult/child one way $30/20, round-trip $48/35).

Bob Hope/ Burbank Airport

Domestic flights operated by Alaska, American, Southwest, United and other major US airlines also arrive at **Bob Hope/ Burbank Airport** (BUR; www.burbankairport.com; 2627 N Hollywood Way, Burbank), located about 14 miles northwest of

downtown LA. It's handy if you're headed for Hollywood, Downtown or Pasadena.

Long Beach Airport

To the south, on the border with Orange County, the small **Long Beach Airport** (LGB; www.lgb.org; 4100 Donald Douglas Dr, Long Beach) is convenient for Disneyland and is served by Alaska, US Airways and Jet Blue.

Union Station

Amtrak (☎800-872-7245; www.amtrak.com), America's national rail service, rolls into Los Angeles at historic **Union Station** (☎800-872-7245; www.amtrak.com; 800 N Alameda St), located downtown.

Greyhound Bus Terminal

Greyhound operates extensive, if slow, routes

Travel Passes

The **Metro Transit Authority** (MTA; ☎323-466-3876; www.metro.net; fares from $1.75) operates about 200 bus lines as well as seven Metro Rail lines. A plastic, rechargeable Transit Access Pass can be used throughout the county in addition to cash. Currently, the MTA sells weekly passes ($25), valid on both bus and rail lines. Tickets and passes are sold at more than 400 retail outlets around town, and at MTA customer centers including **Union Station** (⏱6am-6:30pm Mon-Fri) and **Mid-City** (5301 Wilshire Blvd; ⏱9am-5pm Mon-Fri).

cross North America. Its ain Los Angeles termi- al is **downtown** (☎ 213-29-8401; www.greyhound. m; 1716 E 7th St). Avoid riving after dark.

Getting Around

lthough having a car preferable, if you onfine your excursions the Hollywood–Los eliz–Downtown swirl ou can do just fine with e Metro Red Line. And s only a moderate ride om West Hollywood nd Beverly Hills to Santa onica aboard buses quipped with bike racks. ring a bicycle and your iobility and possibilities xpand.

us

☑ **Best for...** Trave- ng between different eighborhoods.

A network of bus routes ans the metropolis, ith most operated by **etro Transit Authority** MTA; ☎ 323-466-3876; www. etro.net; fares from $1.75). s one-way fare starts $1.75. Most routes

operate 5am to 2am daily. Individual tickets (exact fare required) can be purchased from the bus driver.

➡ Fast, frequent Metro Rapid buses (numbered in the 700s) make limited stops. Bus 720 travels downtown from Santa Monica via Westwood, Beverly Hills and Mid-City's Miracle Mile along Wilshire in about 45 to 90 minutes, depending on departure time.

Big Blue Bus

➡ Santa Monica's **Big Blue Bus** (☎ 310-451-5444; www.bigbluebus.com; fares from $1) rumbles through much of western LA including Beverly Hills, Culver City, Westwood/ UCLA and Venice.

➡ One-way fares are $1 and transfers to a differ- ent bus or bus system are 50¢. The freeway express to Downtown LA costs $2 (from another bus, transfer is $1).

➡ We abbreviate Big Blue Bus routes as 'BBB.'

Car & Motorcycle

☑ **Best for...** Getting around under your own steam and grappling with the traffic like a local.

➡ If you're planning to visit several neighbor- hoods, it may be wise to rent a car. Because of LA's sprawl, public transportation can be cumbersome and time- consuming, while taxis can be expensive.

➡ Rental rates start at about $35 a day or from $125 a week for unlimited mileage, exclusive of taxes and insurance.

➡ LA's freeways are variously referred to by number or by name. To add to the fun, the same freeway may have a dif- ferent name in a different region. Here are the biggies:

I-5 Golden State/Santa Ana Fwy

I-10 Santa Monica/San Bernardino Fwy

I-110 Pasadena/ Harbor Fwy

I-405 San Diego Fwy

I-710 Long Beach Fwy

US 101 Hollywood/ Ventura Fwy

Hwy 1 Pacific Coast Hwy (PCH)

➡ Freeways should be avoided during rush hour (5am to 9am and 3pm to 7pm), although traffic jams can occur at any

Transportation Within Los Angeles

	Burbank	Downtown	Hollywood	LAX	Long Beach	Pasadena	Santa Monica
Burbank		Metro Red Line 20min	Metro Red Line 4min	car 1hr	car 1hr-90min	car 30min	car 1hr
Downtown	Metro Red Line 20min		Metro Red Line 15min	Flyaway shuttle 45min-1hr	Metro Blue Line 53min	Metro Gold Line 25min	Big Blue Bus 10 40-90min
Hollywood	Metro Red Line 4min	Metro Red Line 15min		car 45min-1hr	car 90min	car 35-45min	car 45min-1hr
LAX	car 1hr	Flyaway shuttle 45min-1hr	car 45min-1hr		car 45min	car 40min-1hr	car 20-30min
Long Beach	car 1hr-90min	Metro Blue Line 53min	car 90min	car 45min		car 45min	car 45min
Pasadena	car 30min	Metro Gold Line 25min	car 35-45min	car 40min-1hr	car 45min		car 40min
Santa Monica	car 1hr	Big Blue Bus 10 40-90min	car 45min-1hr	car 20-30min	car 45min	car 40min	

time. Waze is the best smartphone mapping service. It factors existing traffic into its suggested route to get you there as quickly as possible.

➡ Street parking spots may be metered or restricted, so obey posted signs to avoid a ticket. Private lots and parking garages cost at least $5 a day and can be more expensive downtown. Valet parking at hotels can cost as much as $40 a day.

➡ Municipal lots near Rodeo Dr in Beverly Hills and bordering Third St Promenade in Santa Monica are free for two hours.

Driver's License
Visitors can legally drive in California with a valid driver's license issued in their home country. An International Driving Permit is not compulsory.

Metro Rail

☑ **Best for...** Traveling between downtown, the Valley, Hollywood, Culver City and Exposition Park.

➡ Operated by MTA, Metro subway and light-rail trains connect downtown with Hollywood, Los Feliz and Universal City (Red Line), Pasadena (Gold Line) LAX (Green Line), Long Beach (Blue Line) and Korea Town (Purple Line).

➡ One-way fares on most trains are $1.50. Silver Line trains cost $2.45.

➡ Trains run from approximately 5am to midnight.

axi

Best for... short hops
thin contained neigh-
rhoods. Crosstown
bs cost your firstborn.

ost companies charge
$2.85 base fee then
.70 per mile. Costs can
d up quickly in traffic-
arled LA. Surcharges
airport trips may
ply.

verly Hills Cab Co
(☎800-273-6611; www.
verlyhillscabco.com)

hecker Cab (☎800-300-
07; http://ineedtaxi.com)

xi Taxi (☎310-444-4444;
w.santamonicataxi.com) In
nta Monica.

ber (www.uber.com) The
p-based driver service,
hugely popular here
d is a nice alternative
taxis.

ssential
nformation

usiness Hours

Normal business hours
e 9am to 5pm Monday
Friday. Banks usually
en from 8:30am to
30pm Monday to

Thursday and to 5:30pm
on Friday; some also
open from 9am to 2pm
on Saturday.

➡ Shops open from 10am
to 7pm Monday to Sat-
urday, though shopping
malls may close later, and
open from 11am to 6pm
on Sunday.

➡ Bars are generally open
from late afternoon until
2am.

➡ Restaurants generally
serve lunch from 11am
to 3pm and dinner from
5:30pm to 10pm.

Electricity

120V/60Hz

120V/60Hz

Emergency

Police, Fire, Ambulance
(☎911)

**Rape & Battering
Hotline** (☎310-392-8381,
213-626-3393; ⊙24hr)

**Rape Treatment Center,
UCLA** (☎310-319-4503)

Public Holidays

New Year's Day
January 1

**Martin Luther King Jr
Day** Third Monday in
January

Presidents' Day Third
Monday in February

Easter A Friday and Sunday in March or April

Memorial Day Last
Monday in May

Independence Day
July 4

Labor Day First Monday in September

Columbus Day Second Monday in October

Veterans' Day November 11

Thanksgiving Fourth Thursday in November

Christmas Day December 25

Safe Travel

➡ Traffic accidents are your biggest threat in Los Angeles, so make sure to buckle up, even in a taxi. It's actually the law in California. Take care not to drink and drive; designate a driver.

➡ Violent crime is mostly confined to well-defined areas of East LA and South LA, as well as less-trafficked blocks in Hollywood, Venice and downtown. Avoid these areas after dark. Downtown is the site of 'Skid Row,' an area roughly bounded by 3rd, Alameda, 7th and Main, where many of the city's homeless spend the night.

Telephone

US cell phones operate on GSM 1900. If your home country uses a different standard, you'll need a multiband GSM phone to make calls and access data in LA. If you have an unlocked multi-band phone, a prepaid rechargeable SIM chip is usually cheaper than using your own network. You can also buy inexpensive pay-as-you-go phones.

City Codes

All California phone numbers consist of a three-digit area code followed by a seven-digit local number. Even local calls from cell phones require the entire number to be dialed. Toll-free numbers start with ☎800, 866, 877 or 888.

Anaheim (☎657, ☎714)

Beverly Hills, Culver City, Malibu, Santa Monica, South Bay (☎310, 424)

Burbank (☎747, 818)

Echo Park & Downtown LA (☎213)

Hollywood, Los Feliz, Mid-City, Silver Lake (☎323)

Pasadena & San Gabriel Valley (☎626)

Useful Phone Number

Country code (☎1)

International direct di tone (☎011)

International operator (☎00)

Local directory inquiries (☎411)

Operator (☎0)

Toll-free directory inquiries (☎1-800-555 1212)

Tipping

Bars 15%; minimum tip $1 per order

Hotel porters $1 to $2 per item

Restaurants 15% to 20%; tip may be include as a 'service charge' on bill for large groups

Taxis 10% to 15%

Valet parking $2 to $3

Tourist Informatic

The main tourist offices are downtown, in Hollywood and at the Los Angeles Convention.

Downtown LA Visitor Ir formation Center (http:. discoverlosangeles.com; 80 N Alameda St, Union Station ⏰9am-5pm Mon-Fri) This

located between 7th St
nd Wilshire.

**ollywood Visitor Infor-
ation Center** (☎323-
7-6412; http://discover
sangeles.com; Hollywood
Highland complex, 6801
llywood Blvd, Hollywood;
10am-10pm Mon-Sat, to
m Sun) In the Dolby
heatre walkway.

**os Angeles Convention
Visitors Bureau**
☎ 800-228-2452, 213-624-
00; www.lacvb.com) Pro-
des maps, brochures
d lodging information
us tickets to theme
arks and attractions.

ravelers with
isabilities

Under current law, pub-
 buildings, restrooms
d transportation (bus-
, trains and taxis) are
quired to be wheelchair
ccessible. Larger hotels
d motels have rooms
signed for guests with
disability.

For para-transit and
oor-to-door services,

contact **Access Services
Incorporated** (☎800-827-
0829; www.asila.org). Check
with individual car- rental
agencies for hand-
controlled vehicles or
vans with wheelchair lifts.
Wheelers (☎800-456-1371;
www.wheelersvanrentals.
com) specializes in these
vehicles. You must have a
permit for parking at blue
curbs and specially desig-
nated spots in public lots.

➡ If you need assistance
in LA, contact **LA County
Commission on Disabili-
ties** (☎213-974-1053, TTY
213-974-1707; www.laccod.
org). On its website, the
**Society for Accessible
Travel & Hospitality**
(TTY; ☎212-447-7284; www.
sath.org) provides links to
numerous sources of in-
formation about traveling
with a disability.

Visas

➡ Since the rules for entry
into the US are constantly
changing, check with the
United States Consulate
in your home country

for as well as the visa
website of the US Depart-
ment of State (www.
travel.state.gov).

➡ Under the US Visa
Waiver programs (VWP),
visas are currently not
required for citizens of 38
countries for stays of up
to 90 days (no extensions
allowed) provided they
have a machine-readable
passport (MRP). If you
don't have an MRP, you'll
need a visa and a pass-
port valid for six months
after the date of your ex-
pected stay, and your trip
must be for business or
tourism. Those applying
for the VWP must be ap-
proved through US Cus-
toms' Electronic System
for Travel Authorization
(ESTA). Log on to www.
cbp.gov/travel/interna
tional-visitors/esta.

➡ Citizens from all non-
visa-waiver countries
need to apply for a visa in
their home country. The
process may take some
time, so apply as early as
possible.

Behind the Scenes

Send Us Your Feedback

We love to hear from travelers – your comments help make our books better. We read every word, and we guarantee that your feedback goes straight to the authors. Visit **lonelyplanet.com/contact** to submit your updates and suggestions.

Note: We may edit, reproduce and incorporate your comments in Lonely Planet products such as guidebooks, websites and digital products, so let us know if you don't want your comments reproduced or your name acknowledged. For a copy of our privacy policy visit lonelyplanet.com/privacy.

Adam's Thanks

Los Angeles is a city I love, full of people I love. LA is home. Still, it's never easy to dissect your own backyard, mostly because you usually know what you're missing. So thanks to Alma Lauer, Trisha Cole, Jessica Ritz, Nina Gregory, Burton Breznick, Tchaiko Omawale, Dan Cohn, Angel Payne, Christine Lazzaro, Liebe Geft, the folks at the Wende Museum, Michael McDowell, Alex Capriotti, and John Moore. Thanks also to all those wild seals, sea lions, dolphins and whales that keep us entertained in the water, and to the LP staff and my cohorts Sara Benson and Andy Bender.

Acknowledgements

Cover photograph: Hollywood Hills & the Hollywood Sign from Beverly Hills Boulevard, Christian Kober/Corbis

Go Metro Map © 2014 Los Angeles Metro

This Book

This 4th edition of Lonely Planet's *Pocket Los Angeles* guidebook was researched and written by Adam Skolnick. The previous edition was also written by Adam Skolnick; the 2nd edition was written by Amy C Balfour. This guidebook was commissioned in Lonely Planet's London office, and produced by the following:

Destination Editor Clifton Wilkinson **Product Editor** Tracy Whitmey **Senior Cartographer** Diana Von Holdt **Book Designer** Clara Monitto **Assisting Editors** Melanie Dankel, Christopher Pitts **Cover Researcher** Naomi Parker **Thanks to** Carolyn Boicos, Ryan Evans, Larissa Frost, Louise Horseman, Jouve India, Zak Lamont, Wayne Murphy, Karyn Noble, Oliver Pullen, Matthew Siegan, Tony Wheeler

See also separate subindexes for:

✪ **Eating p189**

✪ **Drinking p190**

✪ **Entertainment p191**

✪ **Shopping p191**

ndex

🍴 Eating

Our Writer

Adam Skolnick

Adam Skolnick has written about travel, culture, health, sports, human rights and the environment for Lonely Planet, *New York Times, Outside, Men's Health, Travel & Leisure,* Salon.com, BBC.com and ESPN.com. He has authored or co-authored 26 Lonely Planet guidebooks. You can read more of his work at www.adamskolnick.com. Find him on Twitter and Instagram (@adamskolnick).

Published by Lonely Planet Publications Pty Ltd
ABN 36 005 607 983
4th edition – Dec 2014
ISBN 978 1 7422 0877 0
© Lonely Planet 2014   Photographs © as indicated 2014
10 9 8 7 6 5 4 3
Printed in China